Mommy Can We Have a Jellyfish?

ROMI BRENNER

ISBN: 0-9798749-2-0
ISBN-13: 978-0-9798749-2-5

Book Cover Design by Deborah Bradseth of
Tugboat Design

LITTLE
SQUARE
BOOK
PUBLISHING

www.littlesquarebook.com

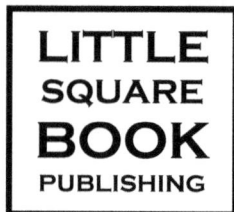

For my little ones and their big daddy.

CONTENTS

A TWO HUNDRED DOLLAR LATTE

It was time to go in for the most humiliating of appointments that as a female, I dread like none other. Although I am a grown woman who has done this many times, it still manages to reduce me to a horrible state of vulnerability that borders on my feeling violated every time I have to go through it.

Indeed, it was time to take my car in for an oil change.

I have decided I have been just as overcharged and ripped off at the corner quick lube places as I have at the dealership, and made the executive decision to be responsible and go to the dealership, hoping to get this ordeal crossed off the list as quickly as possible.

Actually, before I continue, there is one exception to my general disdain for car shops et al, and it is Brake Masters on Ventura Boulevard in Studio City, California. For just eighteen dollars, this amazing team would give my car a full oil change and check the tires and brakes. Even more astoundingly, when I'd ask what needed to be replaced, they would tell me no, the brake pads still had thirty percent life left, I could wait until next time. Or, yes, the front tires were a bit worn and I should replace them now.

I loved these guys so much that when we left California and moved up to Oregon I spent not a small amount of time trying to figure out how I could pack them into the moving truck and take them with me.

I despise myself for perpetuating the stereotype that women are easy targets in auto shops; alas, my knowledge of cars amounts to being able to check my oil, check the tire pressure, put gas in my car and tell if the radiator fluid is low. I once put on a spare but that doesn't really count because a friend was helping me and her husband works for Les Schwab Tires, so she actually did know what she was doing.

I turned off the engine, suddenly looking around with acute embarrassment at the state of my car. There was a sippy cup in one of the drink holders that had some ominous looking goop around the lid, and a filthy, crumpled baby wipe scrunched up in the other space where a travel coffee mug would fear to tread. The whole surface of the console was coated with a thin but terribly sticky layer of crud, the origin of which I couldn't place.

The floor of the front passenger seat hosted the package of aforementioned wipes, a toddler-sized red jacket, a veritable menagerie of assorted dinosaurs and plastic sharks and several layers of glitter, dried beans, pompoms, acorns and rice fragments that had fallen off my children's school artwork over the last few days.

The back seat was another problem altogether. The floor was awash in blankets, sweatshirts, flip flops, small stuffed animals, approximately three reams worth of half-finished drawings and the corresponding dried out markers and broken crayons, and a wooly assortment of lint-laden binkies. Finely crushed bits of crackers and other unidentifiable cereal particles lay in the creases of the upholstery and I discovered a stash of gum wrappers on the inside of the door next to my daughter's booster. There were some dark, oozy raisins smudged across the bottom of the floor covers; whether or not they made their debut into my car as grapes and slowly rotted or were already raisins upon entry will remain a mystery that I will never solve.

While it may seem impossible to believe, I do actually attempt to clean out my car on a fairly regular basis. But to my stupefaction, the stuff just multiplies faster than I can keep it at bay. On the bright side, if we ever get stranded somewhere, we should be able to sustain and entertain ourselves quite comfortably until the rescue party arrives.

I got out of the car as the technician approached me. "Hi, what can I do for you today?" he asked.

"I just need an oil change, please," I said. The

dance had begun.

"Sure, you bet," he said, "Have you been in to see us before?"

"I have," I confirmed.

"Great, we can look you up by your phone number," he said. I gave him the digits, and lo and behold, there I was, all prepopulated and ready to go. He asked for the keys and upon handing them over, I was whisked away to the waiting room.

Ah, the auto shop waiting room. I felt like I was entering a saloon in the old west, an establishment with a predominantly male crowd who all stopped what they were doing and looked up at me when I walked in as if to say they didn't like my kind around there.

The room smelled like rubber, solvent and those all in one watery hazelnut lattes from the coffee machine. Dog eared issues of Time and Newsweek were splashed across the occasional side table.

I pulled my cell phone out of my bag and started checking email. Nobody spoke to each other; the silence was broken every so often by the bang of the vending machine as someone finally got up to get a soda or the whir and swoosh of the coffee machine as someone got another two-spoons-of-powder-just-add-water cappuccino.

After about ten minutes, the door flew open and my tech strode in. He headed over to me, clipboard in hand.

"Ma'am," he began. UGHHHHH. The M word.

The word itself rankled me badly enough but it was also a signal that we had entered the next phase of the appointment. This was the part where the man would attempt to tell me what was wrong with my car and for me to try to pretend he wasn't speaking Klingon.

"We ran diagnostics on your vehicle," he segued. "It looks like you're about a quart low on oil, so I'm going to top it off for you." Like any good negotiator they always start out reasonably.

"Okay, that sounds good, thanks," I responded casually, impressing myself with my cool, calm tone.

"And I would recommend a rain shield coating to help keep the windshield clear," he continued. "Also, you need new windshield wiper blades, yours are pretty tore up." I knew this combo was probably warranted and wasn't too expensive so I agreed. This was Oregon after all and working windshield wipers and a clear windshield aren't a luxury, they're a must have.

Your move Mr. Mechanic Man.

"So," he went on, pausing to look at the clipboard to add some extra credibility to the upcoming onslaught, "It looks like your driveshaft is running at a four degree differential from your timing belt. This is causing the alternator to wobble when the crank is rotated in the carburetor."

"I see," I said, hoping my left eyebrow wasn't betraying me without my consent.

"If we don't replace the constrictive ignition

component of the hydrometer, you will get uneven pressure on the chassis deflectographorator, and this will eventually lead to a blocked flow of fuse partitioning to the discombobulator."

Sweet Jesus. This guy was a pro.

"Do you want me to go ahead and replace that for you today?" he nudged, his face as innocent as the driven snow.

"Hmm," I stalled, my mind racing desperately as, to my dismay, I felt my face starting to flush. "How much do those run?" I called his bluff.

"It's thirty nine ninety nine," he rattled off.

"Sure, go ahead," I said.

SUCKER.

"Yup," he scrawled on this clipboard. "Also, the relay connector is getting a bit worn so I would say we need to replace that as well before the coil wire starts overheating."

I pursed up my lips, trying to appear that I was mulling this one over but the truth is, I knew that he knew that I know jack about cars. "Hmm, let me think about that for a minute," I calculated.

"No problem. You can probably go about another two to three thousand miles before you'll really need to take care of it," he gave me.

He told me he would be right back and allowed me to save face for a little while in his brief absence. I wanted to slump in my seat for a while, to gather my thoughts before the next round started, but you can't let them see you sweat.

Two minutes later he returned with The Filter. Dang! The oldest trick in the book. In my conspiratorial mind, The Filter is the auto shop equivalent of the piece of cake that is passed around on the dessert tray in fancy restaurants. It's not actually the piece that belongs to you, but the one presented delicately to you from a somewhat removed distance to show you what you're missing.

I suppose it might be entirely possible that every filthy, charred, disgusting filter I have ever seen during the pleasure of one of these visits did actually come from my vehicle, and this is the precise reason why I buy a new one every time, just in case. Yet I can't shake the feeling that it's the token filter, the one in the back collecting an unprecedented amount of dust and grime that is presented to every person who passes through these hallowed halls of mechanical maintenance to scare that fool into thinking it's theirs and buying a new one. But how do I prove that.

"This is your filter, Ma'am," he said, with the appropriate combination of horror and professionalism splashed all over his smug face, "Would you like me to replace it?"

I refused to give him the satisfaction of an answer on this one. I just nodded.

As he backed out the door I had to give him credit; he was following protocol beautifully.

When he returned, he brought in the big guns. "Ma'am," he said, "Can you please follow me to your vehicle?"

I leerily followed him out to my car and felt the frown drawing over my eyes like a curtain but I was starting not to care about whether or not my irritation was showing. "Your brake pads are looking pretty worn, Ma'am," he ventured, eyeing my children's empty car seats rising out of the mire of crap in the second row.

LOW BLOW! Playing the precious cargo card. Of *course* I would get new brake pads, how would I risk the safety of my children. This was a no-brainer and I couldn't even contest this on the off chance that this actually was the truth. And worse, even if he had literally shown me the pads, I wouldn't have known what I was looking at anyway. My alternative was to tell him to stuff it and take my car somewhere for a second opinion.

However, I have no free time as it is, and was not in the position to waste any more of it flitting about from one auto shop to another, to prove that this man was trying to retire off my most blatant display of ignorance. By a shocking coincidence, there was very conveniently a buy three get one free sale on brake pads going on right then, so I added this to my running tab of expenditures.

He had the balls to consult the clipboard again.

"Your alignment is off. We can take care of that too if you like?" he continued.

I almost laughed out loud. They would be in there anyway, putting the new brake pads on and again, I shuttle my kids around in this car for God's sake. "Okay," I said glumly, and I thought I actually heard my credit card shout, "What are you doing??" from the inside of my bag.

I was about to go back into the waiting room when my dear salesman asked if I wanted to upgrade to synthetic oil for just six dollars and ninety five cents.

Aaaaand he had just crossed the line. I was done.

In fact, at this point, if my very steering wheel had fallen off I would have walked home rather than purchase a replacement from this man.

I retreated to the safety of the java scented waiting room and sat down, slightly disoriented and confused. I knew I had just been swindled, as usual, but couldn't prove a thing, and worse, I had consented to it all. What a perfect racket.

I paid in a blurred haze and was guided back to the driver's side door. I slowly got in and reoriented myself with my car, adjusted the mirrors and pulled the seat forward. It was only when I turned on the ignition and *Fruit Salad* came blaring through the speakers that I realized I had been rocking out to The Wiggles on the way over there. *By myself.* I wondered how often they changed the filter of the big red car.

My irritation grew steadily on the way home and my husband's reaction to this interchange didn't do anything to quell my ire.

"What?! What the hell kind of oil change did you get for two hundred sixty eight, ninety five?" he retorted, his face a study in incredulity as he reviewed the invoice.

"Well I don't know!" I snapped. "That's why I wish you would just take my car in for me!"

"You're a smart person, Romi," he countered. "Didn't that sound excessive to you?"

"Listen, if you need me to fix an Excel formula for you, I can, if you need me to make a school lunch in under fifty seconds, I can, if you want me to help you edit a presentation or write an SQL query, just say the word. But this is totally out of my depth! I have a broken discombobulator!" I snarled, "I don't even know what that is!!"

He looked at me for a moment, and then just shook his head. "Boy, they saw you coming," he muttered.

"Yes! Yes of course they did," I huffed.

Next time though, they will see YOU coming my friend, because I refuse to subject myself to this nonsense again. Just as no husband should have to go to the store to buy tampons for his wife, no wife should have to take the family car in for an oil change.

And if that's a step back for feminism in our time, so be it. Besides I bet Rosie the Riveter knew how to replace her own drive shaft.

So game, set and match for you, Mr. Mechanic. Well played. Good luck selling a wobbling carburetor tune up to big daddy Russ next time. I'd almost want to go with him just to see that. From the waiting room, with a big bag of popcorn and a two-spoons-of-powder-just-add-water hazelnut latte, of course.

SPECK

I had almost finished drying my daughter's long, thick mane. This had taken a good twenty minutes and it was now going on eight o'clock at night. We were right on track for bedtime. Despite its loud volume, the whir of the hairdryer was strangely hypnotically soothing, and we were both lost in thought, Mia making faces at herself in the mirror while I pulled up a small segment of hair at a time with one hand, blow drying it with the other.

As I pulled up a section from the back, a tiny whitish speck caught my eye. I peered at it more closely, squinting a little. Just a speck of dandruff, right? I pinched it with my forefinger and thumb and when I pulled that strand of hair through my fingers, the speck was still there on the strand, a few inches down from her scalp. My heart started beating a little faster but I didn't want to panic Mia. Maybe it was just some glue from a school craft project or something.

I pulled another section, smaller than before and scrutinized it thoroughly. I saw another teardrop shaped speck, and then another, and then my blood ran cold.

Sometimes I wonder how people know what something is when they encounter it for the first time, having never seen or experienced it before. It amazes me how they would be so sure of something they had never had any prior contact with, but now I understand. You just know.

Because, while I had never seen lice before in my thirty six years, I knew, with every cell of my horrified being, that this was it.

I wanted to shriek and bolt out of the bathroom but when you're the parent you don't get to do that. I switched off the hairdryer and calmly told my daughter that I'd be right back.

I hefted my eight months along pregnant self upstairs as fast as my swollen legs could carry me and burst into the home office where my husband was sitting in front of the computer.

Putting my hand on his shoulder, I tried to break it as quietly as I could so that my poor daughter didn't hear the hysteria in my voice that was welling up in my throat. "Mia has lice," I said, speaking the terrible truth for the first time out loud.

"WHAT?!" spat Russell. My husband is not an alarmist. He is not a type A, rush around, scurry about to get somewhere type of person. But he leapt up like the seat of his pants had just caught alight and before I could even say another word, threw his shoes on and raced to the garage. I caught something about Rite Aid as he blazed past me on his way out the door.

I lumbered downstairs to find my daughter. She was sitting innocently in the living room, sketching on a pad of paper. Now that I thought about it, she had been scratching her head a lot lately. I'd actually checked for lice a few weeks back but hadn't seen any.

I googled lice and the warning signs included redness on the scalp, especially behind the ears and on the nape of the neck. Mia was lost in her drawings and didn't even notice me moving her hair aside. I was so hoping not to see it, so hoping that this was just me overreacting and we could call it a night, but in the pit of my mother's intuition I knew it was there. Lo and behold, like racing stripes outlining her hairline, there was the reddened skin all along the back of her neck and behind her ears.

"Sweetheart," I began gently, my nonchalant demeanor at sixes and sevens with my inner freak out, "We're going to have to wash your hair again tonight."

Mia frowned. "Why?" she said.

"Well, you have little bugs in your hair," I continued, willing myself not to dance the involuntary jig of shivers that seem to take over my body when something gives me the creeps. "Daddy's gone to get you some special shampoo that we have

15

to use and then we'll have to wash it out again."

"BUGS?" Mia cried, wide-eyed and lost.

"They're called lice, my love," I confirmed. "It just happens sometimes," was my attempt to reassure her, not to mention myself, "But we'll get them out and then everything will be fine."

"Oh. Okay," she said, and went back to her drawing.

Just then the garage door rolled up, and I heard the roar of the engine as Russell screeched into the driveway.

He burst into the house, flinging a bag into my hand like he was passing the baton in a relay race. Digging around in the loot contained within, it looked as though he must have run alongside the aisle sweeping any and all lice related products into the cart. The only items that appeared to have escaped his panicked grasp was a hazmat suit and the sort of tenting that one puts up around a house that has a termite infestation.

"The pharmacist said this was a good one," he said, fishing out the box of Rid. "You have to put the stuff on her hair, then comb it out, then wash it. This kit has a comb in it as well, we have to use this one to get it all out. Then this," he went on, producing a spray bottle, "Is for the bedding and stuffed animals. We have to take all the stuffed animals and seal them in a bag for two weeks. We have to wash all her pillowcases, sheets, comforter cover and towels every day."

This last bit of news made me want to cry. I was at the stage in my pregnancy where I was just slightly smaller than a school bus and even putting my shoes on required more effort than seemed warranted. The thought of this much extra laundry heaped onto my to do list was about as appealing as putting on a bathing suit in public.

"Okay, love, let's get started," I called over to Mia. She followed me up to my bathroom and I put a towel over a chair for her. She climbed onto her perch and sat down cross legged, and I wrapped a towel around her shoulders and arms. I opened the box and read the instructions.

"I'll need some paper towels please, love," I instructed Russell. He turned to get them and I put on the latex gloves. Glancing at the instructions again, I doused Mia's hair with the gel and started trying to work it through her hair. The directions said to use about half the bottle but Mia has so much hair, and it was so long, that I just dumped all the contents of the bottle onto her head.

Russell returned with the paper towels and spread them out in a veritable blanket on the counter. We were ready to begin.

I put the comb onto Mia's forehead and as gently as I could, pulled it all the way through her hair. As instructed, I wiped the comb on the paper towel, leaving a smudge of tan nits along the way like some kind of perverse glitter glue made out of insect eggs. I wasn't too successful at hiding the grimace on my face. I put the comb back onto the hairline of her forehead and pulled the comb through again. This time when I wiped the comb onto the towel, there they were. *Lice.* A few were dead but one was still alive, its vile legs wriggling and wiggling in the gelatinous blob. I felt sick to my stomach. I mashed the louse with the comb and went back for more. My nose was permanently crinkled as I pulled the comb through again and again, each harvest littered with nits and empty shells where these disgusting parasites had already hatched.

Having read up about this new subject while I was waiting for Russell to get home with the shampoo, I discovered that lice lay their eggs on the hair shaft right next to the scalp. This is so that as soon as their prodigy hatch, they can feast upon the immediately available skin. The fact that some of these nit shells were an inch or two down Mia's hair washed a whole new wave of horror upon me as I realized this wasn't something she'd picked up yesterday. Or last week. Or even last month.

It took every ounce of restraint not to just break out the razor and shave every last strand of hair off my poor child's head. Moreover, my own skin was crawling so badly I wanted to jump out of it and it was all I could do not to leave Mia sitting there and run off to check my own head. Russell was scratching his head so badly looking at us that he had to leave the room.

And then something snapped. It was nearly ten

o'clock at night and Mia was fading, her eyes were drooping and she looked utterly miserable. As a mother, seeing your child this dejected triggers a kind of warrior mommy fight or flight response. I couldn't swoop her up into my arms and pull her away from these perpetrators. Attacking them was my only option. And so attack them I did. I launched a full scale assault on an enemy so small I hadn't even seen it despite the fact that I'd been literally a hair's breadth from it for months.

My repulsion was instantly replaced with ferocity. I combed every inch of her hair, and once I'd finished, I started back over at the beginning. Eventually, a few minutes to midnight, Mia began whimpering.

"Please Mommy, please can I go to bed?" she sniveled pitifully. As any parent of a small child knows, considering the desperate stalling little ones wage in an effort to buy even five extra minutes to stay up, when your daughter is literally begging you to go to sleep, you know she has hit the wall and then some.

"I'm so sorry, my love, I know it's ridiculously late, but I have to be sure I've combed all the bugs out," I sympathized. I was admittedly exhausted myself; my back was screaming and my hands were going numb but I refused to stop until every last specimen had been extricated.

Russell changed Mia's sheets and made her bed. When the comb finally came back completely, utterly clean, I allowed us to halt the presses. Mia was so tired she could barely stand up and she literally fell asleep in my arms as I cradled her head to wash her hair out in the sink. I dried her hair just enough to get the sogginess out and called it a night.

Russell picked her up and she was out like a light on his shoulder before he'd even put her in her bed. Then, like a pair of monkeys we checked each others' heads. Miraculously, neither of us had lice but we changed the sheets on our bed too, just in case any nits were lurking on our unsuspecting pillowcases.

I was now so tired I thought I would barf, so I crawled into bed as well.

The next morning I regaled my mother with the sordid tale and to my surprise, she recommended a family friend in Chicago who had actually built a business removing lice from children's heads! This friend's own children had had it and it was so difficult to get rid of using the over the counter kits that she created her own line of non-toxic products that were guaranteed to work. I emailed her immediately and got an equally immediate response and subsequent education in lice 101.

Contrary to popular belief, this vermin actually prefer clean heads to unclean ones, and because it is so difficult to actually see a live one in action, people can harbor this pest on their own heads for over a year and not even know it.

Lice is the taboo that nobody talks about; it's the dirty little secret that parents sweep under the rug due to the stigma associated with it. Like all such things, I too didn't think this would ever happen to my family. It's one of those shameful things that makes you feel like you're the only one going through it, yet it obviously happens enough for people to have built successful businesses around getting rid of it.

I ordered my friend's kit that came with mousse to kill the pests, a thick cream to immobilize them or at least slow them down enough to be caught in the comb, and the comb itself: an upgraded design with really fine teeth that were so close together there was no space between them. This was, logically, the only way to make sure they didn't literally slip through the cracks.

My friend stressed that combing, combing and more combing was the only way to really get rid of lice. We needed to wait four days after the initial treatment and do another one, as any potential eggs that we didn't catch would hatch within that timeframe. I had to keep Mia home from daycare during this period and the four days couldn't go by fast enough; we were both anxious to get past this creepy crawly affliction.

The perk to the second treatment was that it commenced much earlier in the day, and having combed so thoroughly the first time, the general duration was much shorter. Just as my friend had predicted, somehow a few nits had escaped my fastidious attention during the first round and I did indeed capture a few nymphs: hatched lice that were merrily dining at Scalp de Mia every day but not laying eggs yet. Since I had found more culprits during the second great combing extravaganza, I did a third treatment four days after that, just to be absolutely sure there was nothing there. And this time, the comb was completely free and clear.

Twelve thousand loads of laundry later, we were able to put this tribulation behind us.

Now came the prevention.

Russell and I lectured our daughter about keeping this at bay: Don't put your head next to anyone else's! Don't share hats, hair ties, brushes, combs, dress-up costumes with anyone! EVER! Don't put your jacket on a hook next to anyone else's, or lie on anyone else's pillow or hug anyone! The thing is though, she was five years old. It's just not practical to expect such a small child to avoid all the human contact that is normal for her age, or any age, which I suppose is why lice is such a rampant problem.

We shelled out for the lice prevention shampoo and hair spray, and braids became Mia's new standard do.

Checking her regularly and even doing the odd albeit much scaled down comb out every now and then will just have to be an ongoing part of our lives, and now every casual head scratch gets serious and immediate attention.

Once you have gone through an ordeal with something, you can never be completely carefree about it again. This wasn't something that just happened to other nebulous people we didn't know, this had hit home and our innocence about head lice was gone.

To keep things in perspective though, if lice is the worst thing that ever happens to our family, we'll be doing pretty well. All things considered, there are far worse things in life! During our attendance at a recent mummy exhibition at the local science museum, many of the beautifully preserved displays included common household items that were buried with the deceased. We were fascinated to see that lice combs were among those items, proving that as a species, we've been around the block with this problem a time or two.

Now, armed with my newfound knowledge, should I happen to see a tiny white speck in either of my children's hair again, my kids can rest assured that Romi the Louse Annihilator is just beneath the surface, ready to spring forth and decimate as needed. Don't say I haven't warned you, Lice...

THE PRICE OF CASUAL DAY

I strolled into work and arrived at my desk at exactly eight AM on the dot. It was a Tuesday morning, and having been off the day before, I was still coming off the high a three-day weekend brings. I leisurely switched on my computer and glanced over at the paper flip calendar to the right of it as I waited for the six minute boot up to take place.

It was scrawled in my messy blue ink and was the quickest buzz-kill I'd experienced thus far. "8:00 AM meeting" was the only clue I'd left for myself. Now I was already late for a meeting I knew nothing about.

It took another few seconds to sink in that it was casual month in Ops. I had arrived for work that day clad in partially faded denim overalls, tennis shoes and a heather-gray, long-sleeved, waffle-knit t-shirt. Although my hair was clean, it was pulled back into a clumsy ponytail and my face was completely devoid of makeup.

Great. Now I was late for a meeting I knew nothing about, dressed as an eleven year old farm hand.

I waited the agonizing six, molasses minutes and my computer finally produced the application launcher. I frantically checked my calendar to find the meeting, for which I was now seven minutes late, was a Corporate-wide kickoff to launch the new data warehouse for our system. I scanned the names on the invitation list and found representatives from our offices in Connecticut, Arizona, Los Angeles and Sacramento, and yours truly: the only delegate from Oregon.

Oh sweet Mother of God!

By this stage, my cube neighbor had cottoned on to my plight. Once you are a mother, you feel the pain of everyone else's child, and she graciously handed me the blue blazer that was hanging in her cube.

I thanked her profusely, grabbed my pen and notebook and bolted for the stairwell. I cleared two steps at a time and had managed to wriggle into the blazer by the time I reached the top of the stairs.

I dashed into the videoconference room and plopped my pen and notebook down on the desk. To my amazement and profound relief, both the monitor displaying the Portland office and the monitor displaying the LA office were blank.

The time between the idea entering my head and my executing it could only be measured in nanoseconds.

I would seize this fortuitous opportunity to unhook the top of my overalls and tuck them into the pants part. Then I could button the blazer and no-one would be the wiser.

I flung off the blazer and threw it onto the table. I tugged on the buckles and they gave way wildly, flying away from my shoulders and then landing with a loud ting of the metal to metal as they collided with the table leg. I shoved the front of the bib down into my pants and they folded away in a swift, easy movement. I was mid-tuck down the back of my breeches when I heard it.

"Who's that in Portland?"

I shot up rod-straight, as the weight of that terrible moment crashed down over me like a herd of runaway buffalo. I could feel the fire of my blood start from my toenails and rush through to the roots of my hair like a bullet. From the heat I could sense the extent of the crimson in my face, and I couldn't believe it hadn't combusted yet.

"You can see me?" I stammered, my voice straining to sound nonchalant in the preposterous hope against all scraps of hope that maybe they'd just joined on the line. "I can't see you."

"Yeah, we can see you," replied the faceless wonder from the other side of the blank television set. "You must be having technical difficulties."

Technical difficulties?! They had no idea. I slumped down into a chair and tried to catch my breath. I prayed silently for the ground to split in a deep chasm of mercy and swallow me whole, or that a large bird of prey would come swiftly through the window and swoop me away from this nauseating situation but of course neither happened.

I waited for the chorus of laughter but IT NEVER CAME.

How long had they been there? Who even *were* they? Did they see the whole thing? Were they on mute while they gasped for breath, guffawing like pack of rabid hyenas on the other end? Who *does* this kind of thing?? Me. Me, apparently. And possibly Bridget Jones. Although even she might have realized this was not the sort of thing one does in a video conference room. Even if the screens were blank.

It was that nightmare where you get to work wearing only a barrel except I was painfully awake.

The utterly horrifying part was that after several more minutes, other folks began experiencing technical difficulties too, and half an hour into the three hour meeting they called it a day and it was all for naught.

I can attest that it has been a number of years since this unfortunate lapse in judgment for which I was miraculously neither fired nor reprimanded. I now have the privilege of working from a home office where (I think?!) nobody can see me in my yoga pants and tank top.

I will never know who was watching me frantically rearranging the overalls bib in my pants that day but all I can say is there is no measure for the depths of my gratitude that it occurred in the innocent time before YouTube and Facebook; a time when you could do something so outrageously stupid as start to undress in a conference room before a live meeting and not have the recorded evidence splashed out in front of the whole world. A time when such an outlandish display would be remembered only by the unknown countless people watching on the other side of a misleadingly blank television set.

HOW TO LEAVE THE HOUSE WITH A TODDLER

As with everything in parenting, it's all just a phase, and every time you think you've mastered some aspect of it, the game changes abruptly and you are reminded yet again that everything you thought you knew is basically null and void and you are but a novice with so much more to learn.

I learned never ever to judge another parent for being late, because as I soon found out, the weary bags under their eyes when they finally did show up did not do justice to the epic battle they had freshly waged. Their drooping shoulders did not let on that actually, due to the ensuing circus described below, the fact that they'd actually arrived prior to the end of the event at all was in itself no small miracle.

After I'd finally worked out how much effort it would take to leave the house once I had babies and had my routine down, my babies became toddlers and the whole thing reset again; the ante upped dramatically and stacked magnificently against me.

My comfort zone preparation skills were effectively obsolete, and leaving the house now began to go a little something like this...

Begin the festivities at T minus three hours.

Shower while both children come in and out of the bathroom freely to switch the light off and on, off, on, and pull all the dental floss out of the little plastic dispenser, and to ask where their iPad is, can you please draw Mickey Mouse on the shower door, can you help them find some pants, why has your stomach fallen down and why is your butt so big.

Attempt to put on makeup and blow dry hair while kids bicker over everything they play with, stopping approximately every four seconds to break up the fight when the screaming is loud enough to hear over the hair dryer.

Ask your older child to brush her hair.

Give your kids some lunch and prepare a snack to take along in your bag so that when you get to your destination and there is nothing your children like to eat, at least they will have something to tide them over until you get home.

Tell your children to brush their teeth.

Older child rolls her eyes and asks if she has to.

Assure her that yes, she does, and march both kids upstairs to their bathroom.

Toddler races ahead and hides in the linen closet.

Pry the linen closet doors open and extricate flailing child.

Brush toddler's cheeks, nose, eyebrow, chin and occasional molar as he tosses his head from side to side to avoid the toothbrush.

Notice your older child's hair still looks like that of a scarecrow.

Ask older child to brush her hair.

Get yourself dressed.

Go to the guest bedroom/office and open the closet to find the box of wrapping paper.

Choose the appropriate design and matching bow.

Toddler has wriggled around your legs and found a box of packing peanuts on the floor of the closet.

Toddler hastily pulls box out of the closet.

Turn around to grab the box but discover you are too late.

Watch the show as packing peanuts flutter through the air and coat every corner of the room.

Get toddler to help you pick them all up.

Stop every six seconds to take them out of his mouth.

Begin to wrap the present. (Note: this task could probably be done the night or two before but personal experience has shown that toddler will find the gift, tear all the wrapping off it and start opening the box to see what it is, thus necessitating the wrapping procedure to be done twice.)

Toddler wants to help.

Look at his sweet, hopeful little face and feel your heart melt.

Tell the toddler he can help stick the tape on the wrapping paper.

Cut the paper to size and stick a small piece of tape on the edges to hold it steady.

Put the scissors up on the top shelf of the closet so that the toddler won't try to use it and hurt himself.

Toddler has pulled most of the tape out of the dispenser and it is strewn all over the table like a sticky unraveled garden hose.

Tear little pieces from the tape mountain and try to stick down the open edges of the paper while toddler sticks large clumps of it randomly on the part of the paper that does not need to be taped.

Try to get the toddler to lie down and take a nap.

Toddler has absolutely no interest in such a notion and wants to play with his sister.

Finally give up trying and let him stay up.

Wait as long as possible to start getting the kids dressed in their nice clothes.

Ask your older child to go get dressed and brush her hair.

Put shirt and pants on toddler while he is distracted watching cartoons so that he won't argue.

Notice older child has come downstairs in a tank top and mini skirt. It is forty two degrees outside.

Clarify that party clothes need to look nice *and* be

seasonally appropriate and send older child back up to change into something warmer.

Meanwhile, toddler has gone into the pantry and helped himself to chocolate covered raisins.

There is now watery brown drool all over toddler's shirt.

Take toddler upstairs and pull another shirt out of the closet.

Toddler doesn't like that shirt. At all. And tells you about it, very, very adamantly.

Offer toddler a choice between the red shirt and the orange one with the truck on it.

Toddler hmms and tsks. For a while.

Tell toddler you're going to count to three, and if he hasn't chosen by then, you're going to choose for him.

Toddler looks at you as if you have two heads.

Begin counting. One...two...

Toddler grabs the orange shirt.

Spend two minutes trying to put the shirt over toddler's head while he simultaneously tries to take it off.

Put your toddler's socks on.

Ask your older child to brush her hair. Again.

Turn around to find your toddler taking his socks off.

Break the news to the boy that you can't leave the house if he doesn't put his socks and shoes on.

Toddler becomes completely inconsolable as he doesn't wike to wear sooooo-SOB-ooo-SNIFF-ooooo-

SNARFLE-ooo-ocks.

Put the socks on again and attempt to distract toddler by telling him we can bring his kitty backpack with toys in it.

Toddler brightens considerably.

Get kitty backpack and also bag for older child with a large, sequined "M" on the front.

Bring kitty backpack and M bag downstairs and ask both children to put the toys they want to bring along into their bags.

Make sure your own bag contains: diapers, wipes, two changes of clothes for toddler, directions to the party, wallet, cell phone, and all the other useless pieces of crap like mangled lipstick, crumb-coated coins, moth-eaten (but clean) tissues, etc, that stay in the bag all the time cluttering it and never being used, but that you need immediately upon cleaning out of the bag.

Inspect the bags that your children have packed.

Older child has supervised the packing process and you dig through each bag to find the kitty backpack has a few Thomas the trains, four pieces of track for said trains, a board book, a bubble wand, and three pieces of Duplo.

The M bag is filled with paper, pens and markers.

Add a few more items to the bags.

Toddler starts crying because he wants to bring his dinosaur.

Go to the toy box and retrieve a dinosaur.

Toddler starts crying more loudly because he

wanted the green dinosaur.

Go to the toy box and get six green dinosaurs.

Toddler falls over in hysterics because none of the six green dinosaurs you chose was the *right* green dinosaur.

Pick up your bag, the M bag, the kitty backpack, the birthday present, and grab everyone's coat.

Turn around to give the coats to the kids to put on, announcing that it's time to put on shoes, coats and hats.

Toddler's face is bright green and he is still holding the offending marker, without the lid on, in his left hand.

Put everything down and take the toddler into the bathroom.

Spend eight minutes washing toddlers face repeatedly, trying to get the green ink off his face.

Get toddler to look reasonably less like he ate the Hulk for lunch and begin to leave the bathroom.

Toddler gives you a giant grin on the way out and you see his teeth are kelly green as well.

Take toddler back into the bathroom and brush his teeth for four minutes.

Toddler's teeth are now a light lime shade but it's officially good enough.

Go back downstairs to find older child on the couch, watching TV.

Turn off the TV and instruct older child to brush. Your. Hair.

Hear toddler whimpering for milk.

Go get toddler's sippy cup.

Upon returning, discover that toddler has unpacked all the toys from the kitty backpack.

Start counting to ten in your mind and exhale very, very slowly.

Give toddler the milk and repack all the toys into the backpack.

Tell your older child to put on her coat and hat, and attempt to put on toddler's coat and hat.

Toddler freaks out because he doesn't want to wear a hat, he wants to wear the hood of his jacket.

Try to put the hood of the jacket on toddlers head but he throws it back off because, as he explains with indignant crimson eyebrows, now he DOESN'T WANT TO!

Pick up all the bags, and head out the door with the kids in tow.

Attempt to help toddler into his car seat.

Toddler shrieks at you because he wants to DO IT MYSEEEEEEEEEEEEEEELF!

Wait three full minutes while toddler scales the car like he's climbing Mount Everest, stopping to inspect every item he sees on the ascent, and finally makes it into the seat.

Start to pull the straps over the toddler's arms when he flings his arms aside and insists on taking his jacket off because he hates being strapped into the car seat with his jacket still on.

Wait another forty seconds while toddler takes the jacket off by himself.

Finally go to click the five point harness into place and, feeling the thick wad of squishy diaper, realize he has just peed and the diaper is totally saturated.

Unbuckle the toddler from the car seat, tell older child you will be right back, and take toddler inside the house.

Get a fresh diaper and take the soiled diaper off.

While you reach for the wipes, the toddler takes off as fast as he can with his pants down around his ankles.

Run after the toddler and tackle him to the floor.

Toddler thinks this is great fun and wriggles up out of the diaper as you're trying to put it on.

Hold the toddler still with one arm and put the diaper on with the free hand.

Start counting to four hundred under your breath.

Wash the sweat off brow while washing hands.

Go the car and repeat steps 63 – 67 above.

Both kids are now safely buckled into their car seats.

Switch on the ignition and back out of the driveway.

Sit there at the bottom of the driveway with a nagging feeling that you forgot to do something.

Did you bring your bag? Yes.

Are both kids in the car? Yes…

Did you actually remember to put shirt AND pants on yourself in all the commotion? Check and reassure yourself that you are indeed wearing both.

Did you put on deodorant?? Hmmm…

Sit there for another minute, trying to remember if you did or not in fact apply deodorant, and come up completely, totally blank. Maybe that was it?!

Determine that deodorant is not something you can throw caution to the wind about and hope you did apply it after all. Being late to a party is one thing. Stinking like you just arrived in a time machine from a feudal village at the end of a hot summer day is another.

Drive back up driveway and open the garage door.

Tell the kids you'll be right back and dash inside the house.

Apply deodorant (again?) and run back to the car.

Start the car up again and head to the party.

"MOM!" yelps older child as you're getting onto the freeway onramp, "You forgot the birthday present!"

Exhale a long slow hiss to prevent yourself from swearing.

Take the first exit and go back home to get the present.

"Oh Mom," laughs older child, "What would you do without us?"

Grab the present and set off. For the third time.

Get caught at red light before the freeway onramp.

Glance in the rear view mirror. Toddler is fast asleep, his long eyelashes fanned out on top of his round, chubby cheeks, his full little lips slightly parted. Older child is staring serenely out of the window, her wise eyes taking in the world.

Feel your heart swell with love for these two amazing little souls.

What would you do without them, indeed.

SURLY

"How much wood *would* a woodchuck chuck if a woodchuck could chuck wood?" I asked my very first ever question of Siri jovially, holding my spanking new phone. It was perfectly sleek and shiny and not even in its protective case yet and I couldn't wait to take the voice recognition software for a test drive.

"Don't you have anything better to do?" she drawled in return, in a devastatingly condescending tone that was beyond frosty.

Figures. I had just been cut down to size by a phone. I promptly dubbed my version "Surly," and after two years she and I have never reconciled. Mia was able to get onto more amicable terms with her, and programmed my Siri, at the tender age of seven, to call her Sophia.

Sophia and Surly have long inane conversations that go in circles until Surly gets that edge in her robotic voice and I know it's time to intervene.

Mia, "Hi Siri, how are you?"

Surly, "Hi Sophia. I am well."

Mia, "Siri, I'm going to see my cousins next week and I'm so excited! They live in LA."

Surly, "I don't understand what you said, Sophia."

This made Mia raise her voice a few notches. She brought the phone closer to her mouth and spoke loudly and slowly, like how some people talk to a foreign person when they think they can't speak their language.

Mia, "I'M... GOOOOING.... TO....SEE...MY... COUSINZZZZZ. THEY...LIVE...IN...LAAAAAA."

Surly, "I'mgooooingtoseemycousinztheyliveinLA. Would you like me to search the web for it?"

Mia, giggling, "No!" A pause, while she gathered her thoughts. "My baby brothers name is Alex. And my mom is Romi and my dad is Russell."

Surly, "My baby brother Alex and is Romi dad Russell. If you like I can search the web for it."

Mia, cackling, "No, Siri!!" Then, finally composing herself, "Siri, what's your favorite color?"

Surly, "I-don't-want-to-talk-about-it-So-phia."

Me, cutting in, "Mia, Siri isn't able to have a conversation with you, love. She's basically a search engine for the web, she can't answer personal questions."

Mia, "I know, Mom. But I love asking her things." And then, unable to help herself, "Siri, did you know I am in first grade?"

This can sometimes go on for a good twenty minutes, usually concluding with Alex running over and tackling Mia, wrestling the phone away and either throwing it at something or asking if he can see the pictures and videos I have taken of the kids and deleting half of them.

Then, the ultimate betrayal. One cloudy afternoon my daughter asked Surly how much wood a woodchuck would chuck if a woodchuck could chuck wood. That traitorous two-timing snake said, *pleasantly*, she didn't know but she could search the web for it.

The thing is, it isn't really only Surly. I'm not sure if it's my actual voice tonality itself or my accent, which is such a diluted South African these days that it's barely even detectable, but interactive voice recognition systems are NEVER able to understand me. This happens everywhere, from movie lines to doctors' offices, credit card companies to airline customer service numbers. Sometimes these are really simple questions too, but I just can't catch a break.

I try valiantly to do as much as I can online myself, so as to avoid these infuriating guardians of the call centers, but sometimes you just have to speak to someone. And, the kicker is, the more irritated I become, the more pronounced my accent becomes which just exacerbates the problem even more.

For example.

IVR, "Please say yes, no, or I don't know."

Me, "I don't know."

IVR, "You said indigo. Am I right?"

Me, "No, I said I don't know."

IVR, "You said Isaynono. Is that right?"

Me, "NO! It is NOT right!"

IVR, politely, "I'm sorry, I don't understand you. Please say yes, no, or I don't know."

Me, exasperated, "Yes."

IVR, "I'm... sorry... I didn't get that. Please say yes, no or I don't know."

Me, "YES."

IVR, "I didn't catch that...:

Me, cutting it off, "Arrrrghhhhhhhhhhhh!! YEEEEEEEEEEEEEEEEEES."

IVR, "I'm...sorry... You appear to be from Mars. Please wait while we connect your call to a representative..."

Recently I needed to track a package. The package had originally been sent by UPS, and neither my husband nor I was home when the delivery was attempted. A signature was required and there was no note on the door or in the mailbox to say this attempt had been made, so I actually didn't even know about it until weeks later when my sister in law asked if we had received the package yet. Fortunately she'd kept the receipt and texted me the tracking number.

I checked on the UPS website and found that the package had been transferred to my local post office in the overflow mail. I went to the post office website to request a redelivery but the site told me the package was already en route back to the sender.

I figured I might be able to intercept the package and have it sent back but knew I would need to speak to an actual person. The phone number for the local post office wasn't published on the website, so I called the toll free number to try to transfer to the branch. It was just before Christmas and the phone understandably rang and rang with no answer. I hung up and dialed back into the toll free number to see if I could get to a person to ask for redelivery. This prompted, and unfortunately I am not exaggerating here for effect, a two and a half hour expedition into the seventh layer of IVR hell.

After the friendly greeting, I listened to my options to make a selection. This is an issue in itself. Perhaps it's the constant lack of sleep or a sad byproduct of my continual state of multitasking, but usually by the time I listen to the four minute array of options I have completely forgotten which button to press and have to start over.

"Okay, let's get started," the friendly voiceover began. "First, please tell me what I can help you with today. You can say 'track a package' or find shipping...." I waited for her to finish her blurb.

"Track a package," I said.

"Okay, track a package," she confirmed. "Now, please tell me the tracking number on your delivery slip." I read off the digits from my sister in laws text. Of course tracking numbers read like a car VIN these days and are the numeric version of supercalifragilisticexpialidocious.

"150293434958600203943452145698547." A few beats.

"A delivery was attempted on November twenty ninth. The package is located at your local post office. You can schedule a redelivery or return your delivery slip to the post office with your redelivery instructions."

Well that was just lovely. Was the package en route to my sister in law or was it at the post office?

I pressed the pound key to try and get back to the previous menu but I was promptly disconnected. I had a few minutes until my next conference call but I really needed to get this resolved that day, before they sent the package all the way back. I rang the toll free number again and this time, said nothing when the IVR clicked through.

This is my typical MO - just say nothing or keep pressing "0" until it finally gives up and I get routed to an actual person, but this nut just wasn't cracking.

"I can connect you to an agent, but before I do, I need to know the reason for the call, in order to route you to the correct person." Wow. She was the ultimate call center watchdog and was insistent that I provide the required information despite my tight-lipped lack of response.

I knew this wasn't going to go well so I went back to the website and got the number for technical support.

My heart actually sang when a person answered the phone and asked for my name and email address.

"I know I'm calling the wrong line, I just can't get through the IVR," I blurted out, "Please can you help point me to a customer service agent? I really need to talk to a person."

"Sure, that's no problem," my post office angel replied, "I'll put you through to the line in a moment."

I thanked her profusely and she transferred me to the queue where I promptly spend the next hour and twelve minutes on hold, listening to alternating Christmas tunes and the smug IVR voiceover telling me my call was very important and to keep holding until a Customer Service agent picked up. (Or I turned a hundred years old, whichever came first.)

I might add that in the time this hour and twelve minutes elapsed, I attended an entire conference call for work on my headset, with the other call on hold in my other ear.

I was getting nowhere fast.

As much as it pained me to literally throw the last few hours of effort away, I had to cut my losses. I hung up. There was only one way to resolve this, and that was to go into the actual post office and plead my case.

Once there, I stood in line for another half an hour. When I explained the situation to the woman behind the counter and told her when the original delivery notice was supposedly left, she told me there was no way the package was still there.

I was crestfallen.

"So, do I need to go back to UPS now and see if they can track it?" I asked in a small, broken voice.

She frowned. "You know, let me just go back there and actually take a look," she said. "Sometimes it takes a bit longer to send them back this time of year."

It was a shard of hope. But it was enough. I thanked her for trying and waited. Again.

I glanced back and the line was out the door now. I had about four more minutes to wait until I had to leave to go pick my daughter up from school. Another minute went by and my ray of hope began to fade. I was tapping my foot anxiously by then and the clerk came back, her arms wrapped around a huge box. I think I actually squealed.

"Thank you so very much!" I gushed. She grinned. "You have just made a little boy very, very happy!" I went on.

"That was lucky!" she replied. "You are very welcome."

I took the package and sprinted for the door. As I zipped off to get my daughter, I reflected on this crazy parcel retrieval.

For all the apparent cost savings and automation in the name of efficiency, there is just no replacement for a good old fashioned person when you really need help.

So Surly, it turns out I *did* have something better to do, and it was worth it to interact with a real live person. It turns out there's no substitute for kindness, and I'm willing to wait a little longer for that.

CHECK PLEASE

Despite my best intention to get out of the office early enough to pick up my children at a reasonable hour so that I could prepare a wholesome dinner for them, I was nearly airborne as I came screeching into the parking space at the little red school house to pick them up before 6:15 PM. While I understand the reason for the policy, and in fact *was* the reason for the policy, two kids at two dollars a minute past closing gets rather steep very quickly.

I ran into the building, blundering through the entry code like a spy being chased by the FBI in my haste to get in under the wire. My kids were already up at the front desk, my daughter singing and hopping around and my son sitting on the lap of the teacher behind the desk.

"Hi!" I trilled, signing out both children on the computer.

"There's Mommy!" said the teacher, smiling. "See? I told you she'd be here." This sent waves of guilt through my frayed nerves. My poor babies, ten hours at daycare is a long day for such small children.

Alex looked up. "MAMA!" he yelled and thrust his arms up into the air towards me. Mia threw her arms around my waist and squeezed.

"I'm so sorry!" I gushed, reaching for my boy with one arm and hugging my daughter with the other.

We said our goodbyes, and children, jackets and artwork in hand, headed out the door. Alex's eyelids were heavy and he was whimpering for his binky. "Um," he whined. "Uhhhhhmmmmmmmm..."

"You want your um, baby?" I asked, desperately digging around in my bag to find one.

"Hm," he said piteously. I found one and was inspecting it to see if it was passable but he pulled it right out of my hand and popped it into his mouth. We got to the car and I began buckling Alex into his seat. Mia clamored into her booster and pulled the seatbelt over her lap. "Please, PLEASE Mom," she said, "PLEASE can we go out to dinner tonight?"

I looked at my youngsters. They were grimy and exhausted from a fun day playing and digging around in the dirt. After ten hours of office politics and "fires" because of projects gone south, I was pretty worn out myself. Add to that an absent husband who was working the late shift, so the dinner/bath/bedtime routine was mine to do alone.

"Yes we can," I promised.

"YAY!!" Mia crowed. "Where should we go?"

"Where would you like to go?" I asked, although I knew the answer already.

"Red Robin!" Mia grinned.

I eyed her in the rear view mirror. "Red Robin it is," I smiled, and off we went.

Although my kids' daycare is conveniently close to the restaurant, Alex was nodding off already by the time we pulled into a parking spot. It was then that I knew this was a terrible idea. But we were here, and I had already promised Mia we would go out for dinner. Besides, it was nearly six thirty at night and it was too late to go home and start cooking a decent meal now anyway.

Fortunately there was no wait when we arrived at the restaurant. Before we even caught the eye of the hostess, I pulled Mia aside and quietly asked if she needed to go to the bathroom before we were seated.

"Oh no, Mom," she chirped, "I don't have to go."

"Are you sure you don't need to go?" I pressed. "Because this is a really good time. Now. Before we sit down to eat."

"Nope! I really don't have to, Mom," she confirmed. I gave her the raised eyebrow, which she countered with a big, earnest nod.

"Okay," I said dubiously, and dropped the subject.

The hostess led us to a table for four and put a kids menu and pack of crayons in front of both kids and handed a plastic menu to me. She let us know our server would be right with us and left us to our decisions.

I opened my menu and started browsing. I glanced up at the kids and found Mia drawing in the white margins of the paper. Alex was chewing on his blue crayon.

"No, no, sweetheart," I broke in hastily, grabbing the crayon out of his mouth, "We don't eat crayons, we only draw with them, on the paper."

"No ea," he repeated.

"That's right. Yucky!" I affirmed.

"Uck!" he said, grimacing, and promptly threw the offending stick of wax on the floor.

"No, don't throw it on the floor please," I picked up another crayon and put it in his hand, and helped him scribble on the paper.

He giggled and scrawled across the page while I bent down to retrieve the jettisoned crayon.

"Nack?" he asked. Sigh. If he was just a little older, I would have told him he had to wait for dinner which was coming very soon, and perhaps just deal with a little whining as the fallout. But hungry toddlers are dangerous people to negotiate with at the best of times, and my main objective here was to eat and then scram quickly, preferably with as few meltdowns as possible, so I took one for the team and agreed to give him a snack.

I pulled out a little container of Cheddar Bunny crackers from my bag. This in itself was a miracle. My bag, which my husband refuses point blank to even open for fear he will "lose a hand or get bitten by the purse monster," is usually filled with completely useless crap. Ask me for a diaper that's a size too small, or a half unwrapped piece of gum with lint on it, or a crumpled receipt that is so old the print has disappeared, and I'm your huckleberry. But if you need a tissue, ibuprofen or hand lotion you're on your own.

One hissy fit averted, I plopped a few crackers on Alex's menu and went back to my own. I heard the slurp of his binky as he pulled it out of his mouth, followed closely by the ting of the plastic ring as he threw it on the floor.

Sigh. I bent down and picked that up as well and hid it behind the happy hour drink menu.

About three seconds later I heard choking and gagging to my right. Alex had stuffed all the crackers into his mouth at once and needless to say that wasn't working out so well for him.

I cupped my hand under his chin and he opened his mouth, the whole lot falling out into my palm. Now, for those of you who are reading this and either don't have children, or have children who don't do this and have managed to maintain a sense of squeamishness even though you've been through childbirth, I can understand how repulsive this must sound. However, my boy's modus operandi is to quickly eject that which he finds objectionable and I learned the hard way that my choices are either catch it immediately or clean it off the floor afterwards.

Just then, our waitress came by with a round of

water for everyone. She took our drink orders and was about to walk away when I stopped her.

"Please can we order our food as well?"

"Yes of course," she smiled reassuringly, "What can I get for you folks tonight?"

"Mia, what would you like?" I prompted my daughter.

"Mac and cheese, please," she began, "And a side of carrots please," she said politely. I winked at her and smiled.

From the corner of my eye I saw a little hand straining for the salt shaker that was, by the grace of God, slightly out of reach. I deftly moved it aside, and ordered for Alex and myself as well. Our waitress took my menu and told us she'd get the food going right away.

Alex was already getting wriggly. I rummaged through my bag again to find something that might keep him occupied and of course found no such thing. He began pushing back from the table and tried to get out of his chair.

"Look!" I said, my voice sounding as though I'd just seen the pot of gold at the end of the rainbow. "What's this?" I held a little sugar packet up to my ear and shook it. Alex smiled and reached a chubby hand to mine. I let him grab the packet and he shook it next to his own ear. Before I could blink he had popped it into his mouth and grimaced before spitting that out as well.

"Mom, I'm hungry," Mia said. "When is our food

coming?"

"It shouldn't be too long, sweetheart," I assured her. But the truth is, each minute seems like an hour when you are trying to keep two hungry, tired children distracted while you wait for the food to arrive.

Mia and I played tic tac toe on her menu. "What should I draw, Mom?" she asked.

"How about a horse?" I suggested.

"BORING!" she made a face. I waited. This was our game. She always asks me what to draw and when I suggest anything, she shoots me down and this catapults her into an idea of her own. "Oh! I know!" she said, and got to work.

Our drinks arrived. Mia grabbed her cup of milk and started chugging. Alex reached for his and I intercepted, attempting to hold it for him.

"No!" he scowled, "Me do!"

"I know you want to do it, and you can, love," I tried to pacify him, "But Mommy's going to help you so it doesn't spill."

"NO!! MEEEEE!" he yelled and grabbed onto the cup. I held firm, knowing that he was going to tilt it back and that both he and I would imminently be enjoying an ice cold milk shower.

He pushed it away and started crying.

"Here love!" I offered him the straw. "You can hold the cup with me."

"No!" he sniffled, pushing the cup away now. I waited a few seconds and held it up again. "No bup!"

he reprimanded me, his lower lip curling.

I put the cup on the table and glanced around frantically. Things were going downhill fast. We really, really needed to get our food.

"Mom?" came the little voice from my left. I turned my attention back to Mia. "I need to go to the bathroom."

Yes. Yes of course you do. I smiled a wry little smile. "Okay, let me find our server, hold on for one sec," I said. I got Alex out of his seat, picked up my bag, and took Mia's hand, and trolled up and down the aisles to find any of the staff, if not our particular server. I finally flagged someone down. "Please don't bus our table, we'll be right back," I said apologetically. "We just need to go to the bathroom."

Right before we got to the door I peeked back at our table and saw that our meals had just been put down at our place settings. Of course. I smiled again. I had learned not to order hot meals anymore when out with my children. The odds of being able to actually ingest any of it before it turns to a lukewarm lump of rubber are pretty slim indeed. It's safer just to order a salad and then not get huffy and impatient as I wait to finally return to my seat.

After three rounds of twenty questions and much panicking every time anyone else in the bathroom had the audacity to flush a toilet before I could get my hands over Alex's ears, we found ourselves back at the table. Mia tucked into her gooey cheesy bowl of pasta and I cut up Alex's grilled chicken and broccoli pieces.   For some unexplained reason, tonight the chicken was still scorching hot after all this time, and I moved Alex's plate out of reach and tried to blow on it before he burned himself.

"Mine!" Alex exclaimed.

"Yes, baby, it's yours," I concurred.   "I'm just cooling it for you."

"ME!"

"It's coming, love."

I put a few chicken cubes and broccoli shreds on his plate and he popped a bite into this mouth. "UCK!" he decided, doing his trademark move. The chicken fell onto his kids menu before I could put my hand under his chin.

"How about some broccoli?"   For some odd reason, as picky as he is, Alex appears to love broccoli, so I thought he might at least get a few bites of that down.

"NOOOOOO!" he screeched, pushing my hand away and knocking the fork onto the floor. Fantastic. I hadn't even taken the first bite yet and he was officially done.

"How's your mac, Mia?" I asked as I put a forkful of salad into my mouth.

"Mm mm mm mm mmmmm," she grinned. "Yummy!"

"Oh good!" I said.   At least one of us was enjoying our meal.

Alex was thrashing wildly to get out of his high chair. He swept his arm across the table, scattering pieces of chicken and broccoli everywhere. He threw himself backwards to try and get out, and in doing so, bumped his head on the chair of the person sitting behind him. There was a brief frozen second where his face crumpled and turned beet red before any sound came out. I was scrambling to unhook his harness and pick him up because I knew only too well what was coming.

Before I had got all the way through the procedure the wailing began, piercing shrieks that rang out across the room from my overwrought little boy. I freed his legs of the harness and pulled him into my arms, rubbing his little head and hugging him tightly to me. I tried to coo into his ear to soothe him but his cries were so loud I couldn't even hear my own voice. I bounced him and kissed his head and he slowed down enough to sob for his binky. Being a second time mom I thought nothing of dipping the binky that had just kissed the floor into his cup of water and popping it into his mouth.

From across the way I caught the eye of another mother. Expecting a nod or smile of sympathy, I was shocked instead to find her glaring at me and my children with unabashed contempt. WHAT?? Where was the solidarity? This woman had just broken The Code, the tacit understanding between mothers that we get it; that we are not alone in this mothering madness, that we know only too well it is possible to send a little person into fits of gale force ten hysteria if it takes you four seconds too long to locate a binky or if you have the nerve to put the milk in the blue cup instead of the yellow one.

I looked back at her from the depths of the bags under my eyes. The light went on as I surveyed her table. Ah yes, lady. I was you once. The woman with the quiet firstborn who has had nothing but her mother's undivided attention for the last two and a half years. The well behaved prodigal child who uses her spoon like a champ, not spilling a morsel, staring in bewilderment at the toddler across the way coming unglued in his sticky restaurant high chair. Oh, the hubris, I felt a pang of pity for this first-timer. I'll see you next time around, lady, when you're here with your second baby, throwing himself around like someone who's just been stung by a wasp and shrieking like a banshee. Enjoy it now, lady, before your tantrum karma catches up with you as it just did with me, and you find yourself on the losing end of a public display of what happens when good patience goes bad.

Alex put his head down on my shoulder and clasped his hands around my neck. I rubbed his back and felt his hot, tired tears soaking into my shirt.

Oblivious to this whole spectacle, Mia was in mac and cheese bliss. Perhaps these kinds of exhibitions had become so commonplace for my daughter that she didn't even register its occurrence right under her nose.

A few minutes later, and in a much calmer state of mind, Alex picked up his head. "Mo milk?" he asked.

"Sure, sweetheart," I handed him the cup, trying to hold onto it, but he pushed my hand away and since the other one was holding him, I lost my grip.

As predicted, he tilted it back like a sippy cup and the milk started raining down upon both of us.

"No!" he screeched and threw the cup of milk on the ground where it promptly exploded. Alex lost it completely and this time, was inconsolable.

"Sorry honey, but we have to go," I said to Mia, as calmly as I could through my frayed nerves as I mopped up the milk.

"Why?" She whined, her face instantly darkening like a rain cloud.

"Because Alex is really tired and fussy, love, and we just need to get home," I answered glumly.

Now I was the queen of all twits. Mia, having eaten half a bowl of macaroni and cheese, and Alex, having eaten the tops of three crayons, several shreds of his paper kids menu and a few sips of milk, were probably worse off nutritionally than they would have been if we'd gone straight home and just had a bowl of soup for dinner, or even a sandwich for that matter. Or frankly, dog food.

Now here we were, already late for bath time, both Mia and Alex were fuming and decidedly past it, respectively, and I was a frazzled wreck.

Even though Red Robin was kind enough not to tell us to come back only after both of my children were either old enough to drive or pay for their meals themselves, I made a mental note to not do this again for a really, really long time.

I caught my server's eye. I'm sure she was watching us and just counting the seconds for us to give the word that we were ready to go. Check paid, uneaten food boxed up and all our belongings accounted for, I gathered up my children and the last few shreds of my dignity and headed for the car.

Alex was asleep before I even backed out of the parking space, and Mia was staring out the window, somber.

And it was a very, very quiet ride home.

PIECE OF CAKE

My birthday cake karma is really, ahem, crummy.

If you've read *Please Tell Me I'm On Mute*, you will know the struggles I had with Mia's sixth birthday cake pops and how they very nearly weren't. My husband was completely mystified as to why I would put myself through the wringer to make the piece de resistance myself, rather than have the nice folks at the local bakery take this task off my hands.

For Mia's seventh birthday, I baked a batch of chocolate and a batch of vanilla cupcakes, frosted them with a quick and easy piping job, and set up a cupcake bar to let the kids decorate their own mini cakes as part of the party fun. As the birthday girl herself would say, easy peasy lemon squeezy.

So this year, for her eighth birthday, when we began the planning process I realized my daughter had inherited - either by genes or osmosis - my penchant for the fantastical.

What started innocently enough, "What would

you like for your birthday party this year, Mia?" ended with nothing short of needing a stage manager to pull it all off. In a nutshell, my beautiful almost eight year old requested a very complicated dress up party at one of the local inflatable palace type places. I reminded Mia that dressing up was fun, and going to a party at an inflatable palace was fun, but leaping around in an inflatable palace with one's costume up around your ears might not be the most practical of ideas. Mia had recently acquired a Cleopatra costume and was basically jonesing to find an opportunity to wear it. I was finally able to talk her down to having the party at the local aquarium where at least dressing up would be feasible, albeit a slightly unusual combination.

The white flowing Cleo garb was outlined in gold and blue trim, with matching gold and blue cuffs and stately sash. Mia desperately wanted to wear her jeweled sandals but they were last season's and didn't fit anymore and it was too cold to wear them anyway. She compromised with a pair of gold flats.

Next on the agenda: the cake.

"Let me draw it for you!" Mia bubbled. Mia is an exceptional artist, so I readily agreed as I knew her rendering would be a really good representation of what she wanted. She scampered off to find some markers and grabbed a piece of paper from the ever available ream nearby.

Her pen and markers flew about the page and within seconds there materialized something that would have been quite at home on Liberace's dining room table. The confectionary extravaganza was white with white frosting (to match her dress of course), with loops of gold, blue and red piped frosting around the edges and around the top in a very intricate design, and ruby and blue jewels and gold swirled decorations all over.

"Wow, love, that's quite a cake," I said.

She beamed. "That's the one!" she replied.

I looked at my girl, who at eight is now as tall as my chin. I hugged her tightly and said, "You got it, my love."

So this year, I fought the urge to bake the cake and do all the decorations on my own. At the insistence of my husband who has had enough of the last minute frantic scramble over the years, I actually ordered a white cake with white frosting from the bakery. I did buy some blue sugar crystals and gold sugar thinking I'd do the decorating bit. Obviously the jewelification of the cake wasn't going to look exactly like the rendering, but I figured trying to explain Blackbeard's treasure chest to the lady at the bakery counter might be a tall order.

When we went to pick it up, we saw they had sprinkled confetti all over the edges and put some noisemakers in the corner but I told Mia not to worry, I'd remove the noisemakers and work around the confetti. We gingerly put the cake in the cart and picked up some juice boxes, strawberries, grapes, pretzels, a giant bag of chips, bottles of water, paper plates and matching napkins and plastic cutlery. We were officially done; the aquarium would supply everything else.

We got home and I carefully carried the cake inside and placed it lovingly on the kitchen counter. Mia had another birthday party to attend before her own, and ran upstairs to get ready. We had about three hours until we had to leave for her party so we were doing well for time.

Alex was growling and stomping around in the foyer, his hands in their monster claw pose, with his fierce monster game face on.

"Let's take your shoes off please, love," I smiled at him.

"ROOOOOOOOOOOOOAAAAAAAAAAAAAA AAAARRRRR!" he bellowed at me.

"Oh goodness!" I replied, jumping back for extra effect. He broke character for a second and giggled with delight at my reaction. "Are you a monster?"

"I a BIG daddy wion!" He roared back.

"A big daddy lion?!" I indulged him. "Oh you are so scary!" He beamed at me and showed me all his big daddy lion teeth. I usually get it wrong. If I ask him if he's a lion, he's a monster. If I ask if he's a monster, he's a tiger. And if I ask if he's a tiger, he'll tell me he's an elephant, even though he knows elephants don't roar. So I just roll with it. "Shoes, mister lion," I reminded him, and went back out to the car to get the rest of the groceries. I shut the trunk and hit the garage door button with my elbow on the way back into the house. Alex's jacket was strewn across the floor in front of the stairs and his shoes and socks were flung to the four winds. He met me in the doorway of the kitchen.

"I hungy, Mommy," he said, his cherubic cheeks showing off his dimple as he smiled.

"You're hungry, sweetheart?" I smiled back. "What should we give you for lunch?" I thought out loud.

"Cuckakes!" he said.

"Cupcakes?!" I retorted, tickling his belly, "We don't have cupcakes for lunch!"

"Uh huh!" he insisted, a broad, innocent and hopeful smile lighting up his face from ear to ear.

"No we don't," I said, still smiling.

"Uh HUH!" he repeated, his eyes twinkling.

And I knew.

I peered around the kitchen island and saw the corner of a black plastic tray on the floor. I forced myself to look around the other side and there it was, Mia's cake upside down in the clear plastic lid, on the linoleum.

"OH MY GOD!" I yelped. Alex was still nodding and smiling, waiting expectantly for the imminent cuckakefest.

My war cry brought both Mia and Russell charging down the stairs, and to be honest, I would have burst out laughing at the absurdity of the situation but Mia's stricken face, with wide eyes like saucers and jaw hanging almost as low as the cake itself reminded me of my place.

Russell failed to see the humor. "What did you do?!" he barked at Alex, incredulous. Alex immediately realized he was in the dog box and raced around behind me where he hid in my shirt.

"Look what you did!" Russell came around to get Alex, who erupted into tears. "You ruined Mia's cake!"

"We'll fix this," I said to Mia, who looked like she still hadn't exhaled. "I promise, you will have a birthday cake," I reassured her. She just shut her mouth and gave me a look that told me she was going to have to trust me on this one.

Russell banished Alex to "the corner" to repent for his crime, and his gut-wrenching sobs made my heart ache for the poor boy.

I bent down onto the kitchen floor, picked up the sorry lot and surveyed the damage from the top of the container (which was now the bottom). To my amazement, the entire cake was completely intact, although the piping was severely smooshed. "You know, I think I can save it," I said.

Russell looked at me like I was insane.

"The cake itself is fine," I pled my case, "It's just the frosting that is smooshed. I can scrape that off and then do the decorations."

He thought about it for a minute. "Well, I guess it didn't land on the actual floor," he conceded. "The whole thing's still in the plastic."

We had three hours. This was a half sheet cake.

There was no way we were going to be able to get the bakery to make another one in time. We agreed to flip it over and see if we could work with it.

Russell is the steadiest of us so he did the honors. He took the cake from me and like a team of EMTs pulling a patient onto a board, flipped it over very quickly so as to keep it from moving if at all possible.

Russell separated the lid from the base and globs of frosting and confetti came off. But the cake held firm. I was impressed! This cake was a fighter. He set about washing the lid out and I started carefully scraping off the smashed piping. I got the cake down to the base coat of icing and it was now effectively a clean slate.

"Actually I'm glad this happened!" Mia said gleefully. "Now we don't have the confetti on there anymore!"

I loved how she could still see the positive in this, and really, it was just a cake. If this was the worst thing that ever came our way, we'd be just fine. Poor Alex was still bawling in the corner, big gulping, gasping for breath sobs, and I couldn't take it anymore.

We got him out from his solitary confinement, and he lay down on the couch contritely and curled up into a ball. Russell tucked a blanket around him and within ten seconds he was out, his tears still glistening on his blotchy cheeks as he slept.

It was time to take Mia to her other party. "I'll go," I told Russell. "You stay here with Alex, I'm going to swing by Joann Fabrics on my way home and pick up some frosting for the sides."

After I dropped her off, I sped off like the madwoman on a mission that I was, and powered through the aisles of Joann Fabrics as if I was on a game show and had two minutes to fill my cart before the time ran out.

Now that I was on my own, I allowed the laughter to bubble out and guffawed to myself like a hyena with a screw loose.

This brought back some all too familiar memories of my brother's fifth birthday party. While my mother might argue and say she is no baker, she had concocted a pretty fine looking airplane out of a swiss roll and some other cake pieces. The whole thing was beautifully iced and decorated with various candies.

Not long before the guests were supposed to arrive, my mother noticed the tail and half the fuselage were decidedly absent. The cake was sitting on the dining room table, and the second telltale sign that something was amiss was one of the chairs that was pulled away a little from the table. She read my brother the riot act about tearing into his cake before the party had started and he sat there silently, taking the blame without a single rebuttal.

It wasn't until she found the penitent family dog retching in the corner with traces of frosting all over her muzzle that my mother realized it wasn't her birthday boy who had desecrated the cake after all.

Also pressed for time and up against the wall at

the eleventh hour, my mother constructed a cardboard tail, stuck it on the end of the cake, iced the addition to blend with the rest of the dessert, and simply served the cockpit to the young visitors after we sang and my brother blew out his candles.

I grabbed some ready-made vanilla frosting in a tub and also a red can full of the frosting you can squeeze out like EZCheese. I threw some golden candy coated chocolate blobs in there for good measure and dashed to the cash register.

Once home, I got to work on my canvas. The vanilla frosting was still too hard to pipe easily and I didn't have time to fight it.

I flung it aside and looped the red squeezy frosting around the perimeter of the cake instead. I plopped a golden blob in between every loop. Next, I took the star attachment off the can and popped on the flat nozzle. Fortunately I am an amateur calligrapher so I turned it at a forty five degree angle and piped "Happy Birthday Mia" across the top in my best Chancery Italic. It was far from perfect; icing is a considerably more difficult medium than an ink cartridge, but it was good enough. I went back over the red lettering with gold edible glitter gel. I used the gel to make some swirly curly cues in the empty spaces around the lettering and then showered the whole thing with the blue sugar crystals and gold sugar.

It was quite a busy cake. But Mia's eyes got wide for the second time that day when she spied it. "I

LOVE it, Mom!" she gasped. "It's exactly what I wanted!"

I grinned at my daughter. It wasn't going to put the professionals out of a job any time soon. But it was the right side up, and that was nothing to sniff at. Most importantly, Mia was happy with it so ultimately I gave myself a pat on the back for this one and called it good.

The party was a huge success and after an hour of feeding stingrays and sharks, listening to our guide and tromping from tank to tank in their assorted princess finery, Mia and her friends tucked into the upcycled cake without batting an eye. I quality control tested a piece myself and had to admit it was pretty scrumptious.

On the next birthday though, I think I will order something simple and have the bakery do the *whole* thing. And this time, I will only pick it up on my way to the party.

YES

Clothes shopping. My arch nemesis. Give me a Home Depot or Crate and Barrel and I could spend all day blissfully meandering the aisles. But clothes shopping? I would sooner do sixteen hours of consecutive housework than have to do time at the mall.

My hatred of this activity is either genetic or at least environmentally inherited: My mother's idea of shopping was to walk into a department store, flap through a few racks, get irritated, huff a few times and then turn to me and say, "Should we go have a diet coke?"

Thus I never learned to find the nirvana in spending hours and hours tromping up and down sales floors, trying on outfit after outfit, shoe after shoe, amassing a veritable truckload of clothes and accessories until it was time to have a cookie or soft pretzel at a food cart and, reenergized, repeat the above until the stores shut their doors. Frankly, I'd rather have a PEDICURE than go shopping. And that's really saying a lot.

However, there is no way to completely avoid this distasteful task, especially with two children who are growing like weeds. It was a rainy Sunday, and I steeled myself. We were going to the outlet mall.

I'm not one of those mothers who sets off with everything but the kitchen sink should my wee ones need any objects of their hearts' desires while we're out of home range for a few hours. This has backfired on me plenty of times, but with my husband working every weekend I am for all intents and purposes a single mother on my days off, and there is a limit as to how much pack mulery I am willing to endure. Of course I bring the basics but if whatever it is can't fit into my medium sized diaper bag, it doesn't come along for the ride.

Yet, when we disembarked at our parking spot, it still took a good few minutes to get everything going. Firstly, because I was trying to work at lightning speed so as not to get completely drenched while just taking the behemoth stroller out of the car, I fumbled even harder setting it up. Then, I tried to get Alex buckled in. Like two opponents in a wrestling match, one could say my action word was "to secure" and his was "to escape."

I lifted him up to put him into the stroller and he deftly curled his legs up to his ears to avoid me getting them anywhere near the seat. I finally got his legs down and before I could slide him into place, he arched his back and threw himself up against the back of the stroller. We went on like this for a good while, me gathering wriggling legs and a writhing torso and him flailing like a captured feral cat until I finally got him seated and secured. I was already in a sweat and I hadn't even locked the car yet. I quickly stuffed the diaper bag and a few umbrellas into the stroller.

We bolted for the covered walkway and the spree commenced. "Okay," I said, formulating my game plan. "Let's go see if there are any more shorts, and we'll see if they have decent shoes, Mia, and then we can go home." As with all my shopping excursions, this would not be a full day of meandering in and out of every store, wandering aimlessly about to see if anything struck our collective fancy. We would come, see and conquer and then flee as quickly as we could.

There is another consequence of my loathing of shopping and it is attributed to my already short fuse just to be doing it in the first place: my free and copious use of the word "no." As far as my daughter is concerned I say no to everything all the time. I did point out to my precious offspring that in fairness to me, she does desperately want every item that crosses her path, and that while I do in fact say yes as often as I can, it is not feasible nor reasonable to purchase every whim or twelve hundred, every time we enter a retail establishment.

A few minutes later, we found ourselves in her

favorite clothing shop, where bling sparkled from every rack and shelf for as far as the eye could see. Mia darted over immediately to the accessories section upfront. "These are so cute!" she gushed, holding up several necklaces with dangling neon puffy critters.

"No necklaces, love, we're here for shorts," I cut in.

"What about these?" she picked up some painted fake nails.

"No."

"This diary with an M on it?"

"No, Mia."

Gasp. "Just this purple feather pen?? Pleeease?"

"No pens. Come on, let's find some clothes." Not even a minute went by.

"OHHHH yeah," Mia held up a pair of microscopic leopard print hot pants.

"Um, no!" I put the kibosh on them immediately.

"But Moh-om," she whined, stricken, "Everyone wears these!"

"Not everyone," I said, suddenly feeling old. We kept looking, her vetoing everything I pulled off the shelves and her making every attempt to sidetrack me into getting every feathery, fluffy, glittery rhinestoned item in the store. We eventually came to three pairs of normal shorts and both parties were satisfied.

We were fortunate enough to make it through to the cash register without a layover on the isle of accessory paradise. However, I realized that was just a mere distraction compared to the jackpot of shiny trimmings right under the cash wrap. It was as if a band of preteen pirates had pillaged every kiddie treasure chest across the Northern hemisphere and stashed all their finds from several months of marauding on the shelves beneath our noses. I saw the stars in my daughter's eyes and braced myself.

"Please can I have this mustache ring?" Our duel continued.

"No."

"This pack of cotton candy flavored gum?"

"No."

"Me too!" broke in Alex.

"No, love, you can't have gum either," I said.

"OH! Please can I have this BFF necklace?!"

"No, Mia! No!"

I had to give her credit. The tenacity of a seven and a half year old is quite indefatigable.

I smiled wanly at the woman behind the register. She was smiling broadly, this was obviously not the first time she had heard this very exchange; in fact, this was probably not the first time she had heard this very exchange in the last ten minutes.

Bag in hand, we finally got out of there and on our way out to the car, walked past the Disney Store. Mia clutched my arm and started jumping about like there were burning embers in her socks.

"Oh my gosh! Can we please, please, please, pleeeeeeeease go in there?" I thought this over. At least there wouldn't be any rock concert groupie outfits masquerading as duds for second graders in there.

"Okay that's fine," I said.

"Oooooo!!!!! THIS ONE!" It was a Princess Jasmine extravaganza, with sheer organza overlays, vibrant turquoise sateen and a haloed haze of glitter. I smiled. It was exactly the sort of thing I would have wanted as a girl. "Oh PLEASE MOM!?" She pleaded.

"You can have the Jasmine dress," I smiled at her. I pulled a size 8 off the back of the rack and turned on my heel to walk away. A panicked little voice cut through the buzz of the store.

"What about the stuff, Mom? It comes with all these goodies! Aren't we going to get all the goodies?"

Ah yes. All the extras. Because it's not enough to just bleed you dry for the costume, the toy manufacturers must cleverly add a separate line of accoutrements on which you must then spend an additional mortgage payment. The crown headpiece with the attached veil, the glittery, feathered turquoise and gold shoes, the gold and turquoise jeweled clip on earrings, and matching plastic gold necklace.

My knee jerk reaction was of course to say no. My daughter is actually remarkably creative and by the age of six was sewing little shirts, making "jungle girl" costumes with fabric remnants and glue, and could have whipped up some accessories in a few minutes. Plus, my husband and I are making ends meet financially but we are not the Brenner Bank of the West.

Then I looked into Mia's green and brown flecked eyes. Fake mustache paraphernalia notwithstanding, I saw in them a hunger that I had not seen in a very long time, a yearning I recognized from my own youth, when I would have gone without dinner for a week to have a costume like this. A costume with flowy organza and glitter. And all the goodies.

"Yes," I said, smiling as Mia's grin lit up her whole face.

"THANKS MOM!!!!!" Mia gushed, "You are the stinking best mom EVERRRRR!!" *Stinking* best. Apparently I had really outdone myself, as this was a compliment doled out only on the rarest of occasions. I would be the stinking best mom ever. Well, at least for the next twenty minutes until I had to say no to something else.

We gathered one of everything, and I attempted to turn the gargantuan stroller around in the narrow aisle. We meandered over to the other side of the store.

"BUS!" squealed Alex, clapping his chubby little hands. In my sons eyes, any vehicle bigger than an SUV is a bus, and the bus in question was actually the fire truck from the movie Cars. I took said bus off the shelf and placed it in his hands. His face broke out into a huge grin and he giggled a joyful, infectious giggle that made the salesperson next to us smile and laugh too. Caught by the mood of my temporary Santa Clausiness, I took another car off the shelf and handed it to him as well. He beamed at me and hugged both boxes up under his chin.

"Would you like me to open it now?" the salesperson was ready with her screwdriver, having seen the exchange between Alex and me.

"Yes please," I said, grinning like a cheshire cat myself, and watched my boy, his eyes wide with expectant wonder, waiting patiently for the woman to relieve the toy of its packaging and close the gap between the box and his hands. "Yay yay!" he exclaimed (Alexspeak for thank you), as the shiny truck was laid into his little palms.

I looked at my kids. Both of them were staring rapturously at their new toys and I realized there is a reason why Disneyland is called the Happiest Place on Earth; obviously a little of that magic is spilled into every package that comes off their factory assembly line too.

As a parent it is my job to make sure my children understand the value of a dollar, that money doesn't grow on trees, and that sometimes it's okay to want things and not get them. I strive to teach them to give to others, and be mindful of waste, and to know that sadly out there in the world, some little girls and boys go to bed without food in their bellies or a blanket on their backs so to be grateful for what they have and appreciate the blessings they have been given.

But sometimes, it is also my job to let my hair

down a bit, and remember that they will only be this small once. I am fortunate enough to be able to do these things for my children on occasion, and every child should be able to experience a dream come true every once in a while.

And so it was that on a random Sunday in June, not on anyone's birthday, or special holiday, or homecoming after a business trip, for no occasion other than to make both of my children blissfully, no holds barred happy for a moment in time... I said yes.

THE MISSING LINK

I have managed on rare occasion to do it. I have actually managed to do thin. I say "do" rather than "be," because to browbeat my body into the societally acceptable version of thin is a verb for me; something I can't be but rather have to ferociously struggle to accomplish.

Like a rubber band that will stretch or compress under the right amount of force but snap back to its original size and shape as soon as that pressure is lifted, so I can eventually wrangle those pounds off for a while. But it is fleeting, and as soon as I let up for even the slightest minute, my body reverts straight back to its chubby happy place.

Being significantly short is not working in my favor either and I gain muscle very quickly. I have broad shoulders and wide hips, so even on those rare occasions when I have soldiered on enough to drop the pounds, I still look solid and boxy.

Even at my thinnest, one hundred and eighteen

pounds and a size four at my wedding, one could look back at the pictures and say I was in shape but was certainly not a waif. There are some medical underwriters in the health insurance industry that might still have considered me ten pounds too heavy at that point.

One night not long after our nuptials, my husband and I went to the Laugh Factory in L.A. We sat near the front so of course I was expecting at least a few zingers throughout the night. I remember precious little of the whole evening other than one particular standup, who was herself generously proportioned but certainly not what I would call fat, saying how thin people are really mean because they're hungry all the time. She gestured at me to illustrate her point and said, "Like this woman! I bet she's a real bitch." I was so elated I wanted to run onstage and give her a huge hug. It remains to this day one of the nicest compliments anyone has ever given me.

And then came pregnancy, which turned out to be a one way ticket to Flabville from which there is no hope of return. Two almost nine pound newborns on my five foot frame was all that was required to turn my stomach into a textbook case of what happens when good collagen goes bad, and the delightful abdominal muscle separation that occurred with my second baby rendered me a permanent resident of Saggy Belly Penitentiary.

Indeed, after my second caesarian section swiftly

destroyed what little stomach hadn't been wrecked from the first one, my only hope of being presentable in a dress is a contraption my husband and I have dubbed the iron maiden. Like the legend for which it is nicknamed, it is a torture device that surrounds most of my body from my shoulders to my knees, squeezing it into containment in such a constrictive fashion that it makes Spanx seem like an old, favorite pair of comfy sweats.

However, in return for the decimation of my stomach and deterioration of my body in general, I have two beautiful children who bring me more joy than a bikini ever could. Moreover, it has come to my attention that Sports Illustrated has somehow managed to continue experiencing widespread success with their swimsuit editions without me, so I pretty much got over myself.

In addition, becoming a mother changed my selfish priorities so I didn't really have the energy to care about how perfect my triceps were or weren't; it became more important to think about whether or not my children were fed, dry and happy than whether or not my fat pants were getting looser or if a college football team might think I was hot. The only energy I could muster up to care about how I looked was just to hope that the fashion police wouldn't hunt me down, chastise me for my slovenly ways and force me to give up my yoga pants.

That said, every once in a while I will hear or read a comment that will smack with that old familiar sting. Those who look down on us lazy lot of thick, Rubenesque gals can't know what it is to constantly swim against the tide of our bodies' natural inclinations to be considered visually acceptable.

Just as those who are mathematically inclined wouldn't know the pain of someone who for the life of them can never figure out what "X" equals, or those who have green thumbs wouldn't understand how a garden wouldn't flower, people who have never had to struggle so vehemently to lose even a few measly pounds cannot know what it is like to be in this predicament. "Just lose weight!" they scoff. (Well, why didn't I think of that?!)

The fact is, whether the fitness gurus and eighteen year old jocks refuse to believe it or not, there are some of us who do not patron fast food restaurants, who keep their calories in check and exercise, who do the "right" things, yet for whom "just losing weight" is about as easy to do as mining for diamonds with a toothpick.

One recent afternoon, the stars aligned and I had a free hour to myself. I was buggering around on Google and for some reason, came across Wilma, the Neanderthal woman who had been reconstructed by a team of scientists and artists using bone fragments and DNA sequencing.

Fascinated by Wilma's steely, determined gaze, I clicked on a link and there materialized before my eyes a short, stocky redhead with broad hips and shoulders and thick, muscular legs. She was war painted (or tattooed?) and locked in a fight stance, no doubt about to launch her impressive spear into the hide of some hapless nearby animal who never stood a chance.

And the more I stared at Wilma's sturdy frame the brighter the light bulb became.

Oh my God. I was looking at ME!

While I am no redhead and the trademark small troglodyte forehead seems to have disappeared somewhere along the way from the primordial soup that is apparently my more recent gene pool, in this ancient grandmother of modern civilization I recognized those compact yet strong, well-defined calves as my own. I found the same musculature that has plagued me in the fitting rooms of department stores and caused me to steer away from the latest fashions, settling for "flattering" instead. It appears that all along I should just have been looking for something in a nice faux mastodon!

Fortunately it appears gravity has not gotten the better of me to the extent that it did with this poor woman, but in fairness, there was no neighborhood Victoria's Secret back then to help in this regard.

I stared more intently at Wilma and became enlightened by the ensuing footage about the link between Neanderthals and early Homo Sapiens whom they now suspect interbred. Rather than feel aghast or ashamed that I found myself looking at a cavewoman who was in fact a mirror image of myself, I felt an overwhelming sense of peace and relief. In fact, one might go so far as to say I was elated.

It's not my fault!

Research suggests that modern humans still have between one and four percent Neanderthal genes. It wasn't just my imagination that my body clings to calories like dog hair to dark clothing, it is quite obvious that this is what it was *designed* to do. I felt positively liberated!

I'm sure many in the scientific community would dismiss this percentile as insignificant or certainly not the reason for my continual struggle with my excessive curviness. But it's good enough for me and I will choose to run with it.

This aha moment has certainly made me more comfortable in my skin than ever before and I am no longer at odds with myself to be something I'm not.

I will never be a willowy beanpole, in the same way a pug will never be a great dane. There's nothing physiologically wrong with the pug, it's just the way he was born. As it is with me; it simply isn't in my genes to be tiny in my jeans.

Besides, I'm not fat. I'm just retro-bodied.

YOUR SANITY WILL EXPIRE IN FOURTEEN DAYS

For me, most working days are an exercise in total futility in which I attempt to actually get some work done while attending a back to back meeting marathon for the majority of the day.

In this unfortunate hero sandwich of continuous calls that typically begins at five or six in the morning, I am the piece of lettuce in the middle, getting progressively more wilted as the day drags on yet unable to wriggle out from under the mounds of sliced turkey, swiss cheese, mustard and onion rings of blathering. Indeed, there have been times when, after listening to five straight hours of yakking, I have literally had to mute the phone, place the headset down on the desk and sneak out to go to the bathroom or run to the kitchen to grab my lunch.

There is a certain nagging stress that starts building as the end of a call starts to loom large. This is the point in the conversation where everyone knows the dilemma isn't going to get solved in the next three minutes. This is mostly because everyone on the call has been through this very conversation the day before, and the day before that, and are stuck on the merry go round of garbled nonsensical corporate speak that includes words and phrases like "level set," "speak to that" and "indicate," when someone can prattle on for a full hour without actually saying anything.

Yet, instead of cutting everyone loose to go to the next meeting, the attendees on the line keep banging their heads against the proverbial wall until the call runs two minutes over and someone says they really, *really* have to drop.

It was such a day when I clicked on the Webex button to dial into my next meeting. I was hosting this next one, so I was already on edge to get onto the line as soon as possible.

Upon clicking on the web link, I got an error message from my company's intranet, telling me that my password had expired. What? I had just used it all morning!

Usually I get those annoying messages starting fourteen days in advance, telling me every ten minutes that my password will expire in fourteen days, thirteen days, twelve days eight hours two minutes and fifteen seconds, etc. How I'd missed them all was beyond me.

Never mind, I just needed to get into the system. I plugged in "Miaalex" and hit enter. I know you're never supposed to use your kids' names in a password but as a working mother of two, it's all I can do most days to remember my own name. I am counting on the fact that I am most likely not going to forget the names of the two people I have brought into this world.

I got my pen poised to write down the combination. You're also never supposed to write it down, but let's get real here; I have nineteen passwords to manage just at work, to say nothing about home. There was a very strong probability that if I didn't record the password, I would have to reset it again by the time I got to log in.

You are required to use at least one capital letter.
Miaalex.
You are required to use at least one number.
Miaalex5.
You are required to use at least one special character.
Miaalex5!
Your password is too similar to a previous password.

For God's sake. I sat there for about ten seconds, wracking my sleep deprived brain to come up with something else.

Zoo5#.

Your password must contain between 8 and 12 characters.

Argh! I was now three minutes late.

Ummm… THINK Romi! Zoo2day#. I waited. Nothing. I clicked on the icon again and the internet explorer stopped responding. Perfect.

BRRRING! An instant message popped up on the

screen from Janie.

Janie: *Are you going to start the meeting?*

Me: *Yup, just trying to log into Webex.*

BRRRING! Janie: *np* ☺

My cursor had returned.

Zoo2day#. Before I had a chance to hit enter, BRRRING! Another message popped up. From Tom this time.

Tom: *Hey! We're on the line, can you still join the call?*

Me: *Hey Tom, yes, I'm trying to log into Webex but my password expired.*

BRRRING! Message from Jackson.

Jackson: *Hey Romi! Are you coming to the meeting?*

BRRRING! Tom: *OK cool no worries, just wondering, the rest of the gang is here already.*

Me: *Hi Jackson, yes, I'm on my way, just trying to get into Webex, my password expired.*

Me: *Thanks Tom, please can you let everyone know I'll be there as soon as I can?*

BRRRING! Tom: *You got it*

BRRRING! Jackson: *Ugh! That sucks! Okay np.*

I got back to the password screen and hit enter.

Your password session has timed out.

I could now feel a vein throbbing in my left temple. I let out a stead controlled stream of infuriated breath and closed the browser.

BRRRING! Janie: *Hey Romes… it's 4 minutes after…*

Me: *I know, Janie, working on it ;-)*

BRRRING! Message from Lindsay.

Lindsay: *Hi Romi, I'm the PM for the new DTX system migration that will be go live next year in Q3. I was given your name as a SME and wanted to give you a heads up that I'll be inviting you to a kick off meeting next week. Please can you let me know what time would be good to meet and go over the VFQ doc so that you are up to speed before then?*

Now I had completely lost my train of thought. Zoo#day1? It didn't matter, I went with ZooFun@1 and hit enter.

BRRRING! Message from Samantha.

Sam: *Hey Romers!!!!! I saw you're on do not disturb so whenever you get a chance, please can you take a look at my email?*

Am I in the freaking Twilight zone. I looked around to see if maybe someone was secretly filming me for a new episode of Pranked.

The screen refreshed and there is was, Fort Knox of our internet security had finally let me in. I clicked on the button to receive a call back.

A pop up screen appeared. Set your user preferences to Central Standard Time? YES!

Do you want to remember your time zone every time you log into Webex? YES!!

Suddenly everything slowed back down to the speed of a snail traversing a garden pathway and froze. A new pop up window materialized, my VPN connection had just shut down, followed by a second window to say that my Odyssey Client, that manages my connection, had just failed, thus I was now evicted from the internet and effectively logged out of the system.

I like to think of myself as an optimist. I try to see the silver lining in a given situation, as I think there invariably is one. And on this day, at this sixth minute past ten in the morning, that glass half full factor was attributed to the fact that I was working from home, and therefore not sitting in my cube surrounded by other people, in the middle of the Sales and Marketing floor at the office.

This was because my mouth opened like a gigantic cavernous void, and from it spewed a string of continuous, venomous, maniacal obscenities so vile and at such a thunderous volume I was surprised they didn't peel the paint off the wall.

I fumbled around frantically for my cell phone and texted Janie. *I finally reset my password and then my VPN cut out!!! Please will you open the line for me and I'll be there as soon as I can? My host key is 5287. THANK YOU!*

OMG! Came the prompt reply. *Yup, on it, I'll start the presentation.*

I made a mental note to do something very, very nice for Janie after this farce was over.

I clicked on the Odyssey Client. It was vacillating between waiting for the keys, then the packets in and out showed up but the IP address wasn't there, so it broke the connection and waited for the keys again. This time the IP address popped up right away but the packets in and out were blank. Then the whole thing disconnected and started over.

This laptop was escaping a hang gliding lesson from outside my home office window by a very narrow margin; the sole reason for which being that it wasn't mine and therefore I would have to bring it back to Desktop Support in microscopic pieces in a trash bag and pay for its demise.

The Odyssey Client fiasco continued for another two cycles before I held my incensed finger on the start button and did a hard shut down. And of course, this was the day that I was supposed to give a presentation to my boss and his boss and my new team. What a thrilling first impression I was making in my own absence.

Next I sent my boss a frantic text explaining that I was essentially burning off some heinous technological karmic sins and was now in the middle of a reboot. He was very gracious about it and told me these things happen, but given that it was now nine minutes past the hour, he would let the team know that we would reschedule.

It took another four minutes before my system was back up. The urgency was gone since the meeting was postponed but the residual adrenaline was still pumping through my system. And now of course I couldn't remember Lindsay's last name, so I couldn't respond to her message about reading the VFQ or being an SME for the DTX in Q3.

I opened my email inbox. Twenty two new emails had arrived in the time I'd been missing in action, and a new conference call had materialized for the second half of the hour that my recently cancelled call had freed up.

I opened my Office Communicator to sign back in.

Your password has expired. Please enter a new password.

Oh, of course.

WAS IT SOMETHING I SAID?

I have a remarkable power. This isn't the usual sort of ability that mommies have, the eyes in the back of the head, knowing that the kids hid the dirty clothes under the bed when they were supposed to be cleaning up kind of power. It turns out, I can reduce a person to tears without threatening, without lifting a finger. Just by using my voice. Not even a raised voice.

Every evening when I pick my son up from daycare, the poor boy is beside himself with exhaustion, and just needs to unwind. Couple this with an absent husband who is often working the late shift and a daughter who is also vying for my attention, and throw needing to cook dinner into this already volatile mix and I have a nightly recipe for meltdown pie, the resulting chaos of which is quite spectacular.

The festivities usually begin in the car on the ride home, when Mia leans on Alex's seat or breathes in his general direction. She is a very loving, protective soul and just wants to be close to him. While he adores his sister, Alex is an independent little guy and needs his personal space, particularly after nine hours of having to share and get along with a room full of other kids. Needless to say this is not the ideal combination. Mia takes his rejection personally and her feelings are usually hurt before we even get out of the driveway.

Today was no exception.

"NO! MORE! 'NUFF! MIA!" he staccatoed, pushing her arms off his car seat. She obliged and leaned back but her head was still against the edge of the seat, next to his.

"Noooooooooo!" he shrieked.

I glanced at them in the rear view mirror. "Alex, Mia's not touching you," I pointed out. "Mia, please give Alex some space."

"How was school today, love?" I asked Mia.

"Good," she said quietly.

"What did you do?"

"Nothing," she shrugged. She always says nothing, and later, when I'm tucking her into bed, all the details finally come out.

"Who did you play with at recess?"

She perked up a bit. "Brianna and Sarah. We played on the monkey bars and stuff."

"That's great!" I smiled at her in the rear view mirror. "Sounds like it was fun! And how about you, bub?" I asked Alex, "How was your day?"

"Goooog," he smiled.

"Did you paint today?" I asked.

"Geen!" he replied.

"You made a green picture?"

"Geen, yeyow, boo."

"Oh wow, green, yellow and blue? That's great love!" I said enthusiastically. "What did you paint?"

"Baby whale!" was the reply, as always. He apparently paints baby whales every day, despite the bounty of artwork in his folder that in fact reveals objects quite to the contrary.

I grinned. "I can't wait to see it," I said.

We rode the rest of the way in silence, and pulled into the garage at home quite uneventfully. But this was just the calm before the storm.

Mia bounded out of the car and headed into the house. I unbuckled Alex but he insisted on trying to buckle himself back in.

"Come on love," I coaxed, "It's time to go inside."

"No! Buckle," he protested. I let him clip them together. This took quite an effort and I have to say I was impressed with both his tenacity and also dexterity considering he is only two.

"Okay, let's go inside. We can do up the buckles again tomorrow," I said, pulling his left arm out of the seatbelt.

"BUCKLE!" he yelled, his face crumpling.

"In the morning," I confirmed gently, and after much wrangling while he kept putting limbs back under the seat belt and I kept taking them out, I pulled him out of the car seat and he burst into tears.

I hugged him while he sobbed into my ear and then put his weary head on my shoulder, his arms and legs squeezing me like a little koala bear clinging to a eucalyptus tree.

We walked inside as the sniveling abated and I sensed this was a dinner I was about to cook single-handedly, holding a small boy with one arm while I used the free hand to do everything else.

I pulled a pot out of the cabinet, and placed it on the stove. I opened the fridge and looked around, waiting for inspiration to hit. I rocked Alex slowly back and forth, humming while I contemplated my next move. Alex started to climb down, so I put down him on the floor. This caused a chain reaction of immediate howling.

"Mama-aaaa-aaaaa," he bawled, reaching his arms up for me. I stretched my arms out to him and bent to pick him up when he swatted me away and cried, "No!"

Oh here we go. I turned to go to the pantry and his wailing got louder. I decided it was best to ignore this outburst and get dinner on the go. Alex moved closer to where I was and hugged my leg, still boo-hooing. I reached down and rubbed his back while I pored over the options in the cupboard. He flung himself onto the ground again and howled even more.

I carefully stepped around him and got the water boiling in the pot on the stove. It had just officially become a hotdogs and beans kind of an evening.

"Cup," stuttered a very sad and broken little voice.

"Do you want something to drink, love?" I responded. Now we were getting somewhere, a slightly more rational snippet of conversation.

"Ye-es" he hiccupped.

"Of course, coming right up!" I said brightly, trying to lift his overwrought spirits a bit. I took out a red cup from the cupboard and filled it with milk. I even found a red lid to match and cheerily popped it onto the cup. "Here you go, sweetheart," I said, handing him the drink.

"No weg!" his face crumpled again. "Yeyow!"

"Alex," I tried to reason with him, "It's the same thing. The milk inside is exactly the same whether or you're drinking from the red cup or yellow cup."

He threw the cup across the floor. "No," I scolded sternly, picking it up and taking it away, "We don't throw things. Now I'm putting your cup in the fridge."

This was all it took. He threw himself on the ground and completely lost it. I continued to work around him, warming up the beans and getting the hotdogs cut up. A few slices of cucumber on each plate and we were ready to eat.

I brought the three plates to the dining room table. "Dinner!" I trilled. Mia came over to the table and sat down. "What would you like to drink, love?"

"Milk please," she said. I kissed her on the head and got her a cold glassful. Alex was still face down on the floor, whimpering. I left him to it and before long, he picked himself up and moseyed over to the table. Wordlessly, I helped him up onto his chair and scooted him closer to his plate. I got up to get the ketchup and squeezed some onto Mia's plate.

Before I had kids, I was one of those people who insisted my future children wouldn't need the crutches of ketchup, butter and ranch dressing to eat their food. Then I had kids. Then I became one of those people whose children ate nothing. Then I became one of those people who gave their kids ketchup, butter and ranch dressing with their food. And they ate it.

Alex perked up. "Me koo!" His face was beet, splotchy red and the tears were still glistening in his long eyelashes.

"Do you want some ketchup too?"

"No kank you." I put the ketchup away. No sooner did Mia dip the first morsel into the ketchup, a little voice piped up.

"Kattup!"

"You want ketchup now?"

"Yeth! Pease." He even grinned. I got back up and retrieved the ketchup and plopped a dollop on his plate.

I popped a slice of cucumber into my mouth and watched Alex out of the corner of my eye. He was diligently trying to pick up some beans with his fork but he only succeeded in pushing them around the plate before they fell off the edge onto the placemat.

He tried again, his eyebrows bunched in concentration, and this time they skittered off the other side of the plate. His lip started to curl and he threw the fork on the floor.

"Not working!" he scowled.

"I see that, love," I responded. "Would you like a spoon instead?"

"No. Kank. YOU." He folded his arms in a huff.

"Mia, after dinner we need to start on your homework," I said, soliciting another sad but this time, more compliant, face.

"Okay, Mommy," Mia said. I winked at her.

We got a few more bites down and then I tried again to offer Alex a lifeline. Unfortunately if he doesn't eat his dinner, then he's up all night because he's hungry. Then he doesn't get enough sleep so he's cranky the next day, and gets too overtired to eat. And so this destructive cycle continues. Some nights I literally hear his little tummy growling when I go into his room when he wakes up crying during the night.

I pierced a bite of hotdog with the fork and offered it to him. "You know," I began, "I don't know how a big daddy tiger eats his hotdogs! Maybe you can show me how he does it?" A tiny smile appeared in the corner of Alex's mouth. He didn't move though.

I raised an eyebrow, issuing the challenge. He opened his mouth and, clawing fiercely with both hands, roared a long, throaty roar. His eyes glinted.

I recoiled in mock terror. "Oh my goodness! That was such a big tiger roar!" I squeaked. Alex giggled. "Now let's see how that tiger would eat his hotdog!"

The tiger promptly folded his arms and jutted out his lip again.

"Come on?" I went for broke and swooped the fork under his nose.

"NO!" Alex shrieked and leapt off the chair. He ran behind the curtains and with a swift swish of a greasy, hotdog-smudged hand, wrapped himself into a drape enchilada.

It was over. He was done with dinner. Mia and I finished up too and I cleaned up the dishes.

While Alex was doing his stint as Captain Curtains, Mia had finished her homework and came to curl up next to me on the living room floor.

I rubbed her back as we sang a few silly songs and Alex eventually came out of his self-imposed exile and wandered over to join us. He plopped himself down onto my lap and I hugged them both close to me. I love these stolen moments with my kids, just the three of us huddled around each other, an island of togetherness in the madness of the weekday routine.

We sang a few more numbers and then I knew it was time. As much as it pained me to break the magic of the moment I had to round up my troops for the next phase of the evening. "Who's ready for bath time?"

"WAAAAAAAAAAAAAAAAAA!"

ON YOUR LEFT

There are numerous reasons why I entered the Avon Breast Cancer 3-Day Walk. Obviously, I wanted to help raise money for breast cancer research. But if I'm going to be completely honest here, this particular fund-raiser was full of other challenges that I also couldn't resist.

This was a sixty mile walk over three days, from Santa Barbara to Malibu. Going for walks is my thing; while I despise most forms of exercise, walking is actually something I love to do. However, walking for three solid days was unprecedented. I wanted to be able to say I could do it.

The other not too altruistic reason for wanting to attempt this event was the possibility that the months of rigorous training required in order to not die while I was attempting it would surely result in weight loss.

Additionally, the *minimum* amount each entrant had to raise in order to participate was two thousand dollars. This too, was larger than anything I had ever dreamed of taking on. I typically feel weird even asking people for the few bucks that they owe me, never mind asking for donations on such a large scale.

Lastly, some people whose identity I will not divulge for the sake of propriety laughed at me and said I'd never make it. That was all I needed to seal the deal. If nothing else I had to prove them wrong.

Several of my friends signed up to do this with me. It was going to be epic.

I launched my fundraising campaign. One of my very dear friends had recently been diagnosed with breast cancer at the age of twenty seven. It was a shocking and sobering announcement and her bravery throughout her ordeal was humbling. I wanted to do this walk for her.

To help with the fundraising she agreed to let me use a picture that had been taken during her treatment; her beautiful face barren of the gorgeous mane that usually framed it.

Now that I had my inspiration, blundering through emails and the awkwardness of having to ask people for money became a little easier. I put my squeamishness aside and just asked. The donations started coming in, along with well wishes for my friend and notes of encouragement that kept me plugging away too.

My fellow walking buddies and I began training months and months in advance, working up from a few miles at a time to more substantial distances. The event had organized specialized training camps to do this: carefully laid out schedules designed to get every walker primed and ready for this grueling yet exhilarating adventure. In typical fashion I failed to truly grasp the gravity of the situation, and my friends and I did our version of the training independently.

The other piece of advice I totally disregarded was buying two pairs of shoes to alternate and break in evenly. Moreover, they were supposed to be good pairs of shoes that cost hundreds of dollars. I simply didn't have that kind of money to invest in my footwear and made the executive decision that my one pair of thirty dollar tennis shoes were perfectly suited for the task at hand.

By the weekend before the event, my training walks had hit the fourteen mile mark. I felt this was a totally respectable number, despite the training regime's estimate that I should have been up to twenty by that stage. What was six more miles? If I could do fourteen I could do twenty.

One by one, for one reason or another, my friends dropped out of the event. They contributed what money they'd collected towards my goal, and it was my saving grace. It was a photo finish with me practically breaking open a few rolls of quarters at the registration table to get to the minimum pledge, but those additional contributions put me on the right side of the line. I was in. I was really going to do this.

In the face of all my general scoffing at the numerous, and seemingly unnecessary, requisites for this walk, there was one thing that I decided to take the nice event organizers up on - the towel rental service. We would be sleeping in tents which we had to set up and strike down each day ourselves. The thought of having to manage a damp towel during this escapade thrilled me not, and it turned out to be the best ten dollars I've ever spent in my life.

Not having my buddies there with me forced me to socialize with new people whom I might not even have met if I wasn't solo. I made the acquaintance of some really amazing people.

We thronged at the starting line, listening to all the instructions; our code of conduct for the next three days. Gatorade and snacks would be provided every few miles. There were porta-potties at each stop and the rule of thumb was that if we didn't have to pee at every stop, we weren't drinking enough. As if they read our minds, they hastened to explain that it was critical to stay adequately hydrated, and the fear of having to use the porta-potties was not reason enough to skip the drinking. It did however prove to be very powerful incentive though to walk as fast as possible. Being number four hundred and three in line to arrive at a porta-potty was not a very appetizing prospect.

Each day was carefully orchestrated and they would be tracking our progress to make sure we reached certain mile markers in time. Any walkers who hadn't reached a certain stop by the specified time would be "swept" by a bus and taken to the end post for that day. My new buddies and I made a pact to not let ourselves or each other be swept.

After some warm up stretches and rah-rah'ing, we were off. It was a beautiful autumn day in California; the air was crisp and the scenery breathtaking. We walked much of the route along the magnificent Pacific, its sea-sprayed expanse undulating tirelessly as we clipped along the curves of its shoreline.

We reached the stops in pretty good time, strutting at about a fifteen minute mile. The porta-potties weren't as bad as we had anticipated and each stop was staffed by supportive volunteers. Their boundless energy was infectious and their encouraging words and high fives made us feel like superstars.

Among us were women, men, mothers, sisters, aunts, uncles, sons, daughters, nieces and nephews. Some of the crowd had pink shirts on: these were the survivors, the courageous folks who had battled this terrible disease and emerged victorious. I was inspired by their bravery and joyfulness, and even more awed by the fact that they were taking on this grueling walk. Some of the survivors still had stubbled heads and no eyelashes, fresh from the finish lines of battles most of us can't even imagine having to wage.

Locals gathered alongside the road and cheered us on. They handed out beaded necklaces, trinkets and candy, gave us drinks and kept us going.

As day one drew to a close, my newfound buddy

and I were happy with our progress, and came in with the first third of the crowd. We got to the campsite as the trucks unloaded. Nobody from my new circle of friends had been swept. We found our tents and duffel bags and made our way to the open ground to find a spot to set up for the night.

These were bare-bones two-person tents, and the stars aligned for me in that my tent mate didn't show up. This pint-sized shelter would be all mine for the next two nights. I rolled out my mat and put my sleeping bag on top of it. I rummaged through my duffel bag to find clean clothes and headed for the shower truck.

This was a curious thing. I had never seen a shower truck before but it was exactly as described, a portable trailer with shower stalls. All that mattered was there was hot water, a curtain, and a fresh towel. It was like being in a luxury spa.

By the time we'd eaten dinner, my legs were admittedly a little wobbly. I didn't realize we would have to continue walking back and forth across the campsite for several hours after what turned out to be a twenty five mile first day. There was a first come, first served massage tent set up near the dinner area. It didn't take much hesitation. I ambled over to claim my fifteen minute session. I awkwardly scaled the massage table with limbs that were getting increasingly more stiff by the minute. The masseuse went to reach for my legs and I halted him swiftly in his tracks.

"No, my neck, please," I interjected, ignoring the dubious look on his surprised face.

"Aren't your legs and feet sore?" he countered.

"Oh, they are," I agreed, "but it would feel so much better on my neck!" This wasn't the first time a licensed technician had looked at me like I had three heads.

I managed to talk him into ignoring my lower extremities to concentrate on my neck and back instead. In the ensuing fifteen minutes of total bliss, I'm not sure how many of them actually passed before I fell asleep, drooling on my arm, but when the masseuse woke me up I felt like two years had just been added back to my life.

I also managed to locate a physical therapy tent. My ankles had never been the same after a few childhood sprains, and they were becoming decidedly less happy with me as the evening wore on. A beautiful man taped my ankles with his special magical physical therapist tape and it was enough to make me want to marry him.

It was early when we got back to our tents but by then I was all for it. We collapsed into our plastic marquees and sleep rolled swiftly across the makeshift village.

The next morning we struck the campsite and delivered our tents and bags to the trucks. Day two was going to be a slight change in pace. We would be walking through the town and its neighborhoods, and only for ten miles. By the time we got to the lunch station, the pain was reaching the point where I couldn't ignore it anymore. I took a little packet containing two Motrin from one of the volunteers at the first aid tent and paid with a smile. I hadn't been swept yet, but I was starting to slow down.

As we walked along the bougainvillea lined streets, more and more people began to pass me.

"On your left!" they called out, and trotted past, overtaking my steadily decelerating form. The uneven surfaces of the sloped driveways were a hardship for many people and the taped appendages grew in significant numbers throughout the day.

The depths of the inadequacy of my thirty dollar pair of shoes was starting to show, and the ick factor of the porta-potties was definitely climbing as well, the real indication that I wasn't hustling as quickly as I had been the previous day.

"Hang in there!" called out the friendly bystanders, clapping and passing out granola bars. "You can do this!" I gritted my teeth and smiled at them. I didn't want to be ungracious. But, being the nimrod that I was, I had not really taken into account that while I had got to a fourteen mile stretch during training, I hadn't done it two days in a row. I really hadn't considered that I was going to be doing it THREE days in a row. For some reason I will never know, the blatant "3-Day" reference in the very name of the event just hadn't quite sunk in apparently.

When I hobbled into the physical therapy tent for some fresh tape that night, my Adonis therapist burst out laughing when he laid eyes on the spectacle that was my stride.

"WHOA. That is the most interesting way of, um, walking, that I've ever seen," He giggled. It was okay. I really did look like a robot chicken. I grappled the table and willed myself not to groan as I tried to climb up onto it. My therapist put his muscled arm around me and pulled me up onto the bench in a swift, practiced motion. All due apologies to my husband who was miles away back in Los Angeles and whom I do love sincerely, but I was developing a hardcore crush on this man. He chatted away good naturedly as he taped my ankles and with a few words of sincere encouragement, sent me on my way.

If it wasn't for the fact that my stomach was growling with hunger pangs, I would have forgone dinner that night. The thought of walking over to the dinner tent, standing in line and then walking around to find a seat made me want to cry.

In the middle of the night I woke up groaning. Still half asleep, I bumbled around for my flashlight as I tried to figure out what had torn me from my slumber so abruptly and then realized that I had simply rolled over. It hurt so much it had actually woken me up.

When I shuffled to the starting line on day three I realized that by some unlikely miracle, I had dodged a terrible bullet. The ground was strewn with people stretching and warming up. It was also littered with people attending to blisters on their feet; some were so bad the entire bottom of the foot had bubbled up, and the hapless owners of these sorry extremities were trying to prick them with pins so that they could pop them and cover them with moleskin bandages. Some people had developed new blisters over the previous day's blisters. The sight of this made me swoon a little.

Day three was going to be another twenty five miler. There was no smile on my face that morning. It was all about just getting this beast of a walk over with at that point. I told my new friend that she should do her own thing and go ahead without me so that she wouldn't be swept on my account.

"No, I can walk with you," she said loyally. "Don't worry, we will do it together." I smiled at her optimism.

Off we went. I stopped at the first aid table at several of the stops. I needed some relief. And, I was getting really sick of Gatorade. It was going steadily. Not well, but it was going. Then we hit the mountains. All thoughts of niceness flew out of my head at this point and bitterness came home to roost.

"Look. You need to go ahead," I told my friend. "Seriously, go. I don't want to hold you up, but I just... I just can't keep going at this pace," I finished dramatically.

She eyed me for a second, and I could see the internal struggle on her face.

"It's okay," I let her off the hook. "Please go

ahead." I added a grin for extra reassurance.

"Okay," she smiled back. "Thanks. I'll see you at the finish line."

"Sounds good," I agreed, and watched her small frame disappear into the herd of fellow walkers ahead.

"Who organizes a walk and makes the last day up a freaking mountain," I muttered angrily out loud to myself, plodding along more and more slowly as the road curled ever upwards. At this point, my feet were moving as a result of my sheer will, trudging sluggishly one after the other. I knew that if I stopped I wouldn't be able to keep going, and I did NOT come that far to be swept so close to the end.

There were people on stretchers now at the snack stops with IVs providing hydration that the Gatorade no longer could; people with faces contorted in pain as they inadvertently removed sheets of skin off their feet while trying to take off their socks.

"How are you feeling?" chirped one woman in an attempt to be encouraging as I slunk past her on a corner. I couldn't even stop myself. I just glowered at her and bit through my lip with the effort of trying to keep the HOW DO YOU THINK I FEEL, YOU IDIOT?! from actually coming out of my mouth.

I arrived at the last stop before the finish line. Finally little blisters had formed on the bottoms of my toes and with the continued pressure of walking, the fluid had been squished out of the original locations and migrated up the sides of my toes. I inspected the tape around my ankles and discovered my legs were so swollen that about two inches of capillaries had burst out from the tape, like filigree anklets tattooed with blood. For the first time in my life, my legs were completely rock hard; the muscles were completely seized.

I stumbled over to the first aid table.

"Hi, can I help you?" the volunteer offered merrily.

"I need some Motrin please," I managed through the blinding agony.

"Of course," he obliged agreeably, and slid a single packet across the table.

I leaned forward, and locked my narrowed eyes with his. "I *said*," I growled in a slow, menacing snarl, with an edge to my voice that even I had never heard before, "I need some *MOTRIN*."

His eyes widened and his cheeks flushed. He reached into the basket of pain pills and pulled out a handful of Motrin packets which he hastily threw across the table at me.

I snatched them up and ripped four of them open at once.

"You really shouldn't take eight Motrin at the same time," he cautioned me, "It's not good for your..."

"I KNOW!" I roared at him, cutting him off rudely as I threw all eight pills down my throat like a crazy coke whore who was desperate for a fix. I managed a grizzled thank you before turning my edematous tree trunk limbs back to the road to finish the last two miles of this misery.

I was all alone. Besides an occasional "on your left" as some smug bastard whipped around me, I was among the stragglers now. It took me an hour to walk the last mile. I had never before had to push my body so hard that it was operating on stubbornness alone.

I got to the holding area where all the walkers had gathered to wait for the final slowpokes to come in. It was the beach.

Sand.

After walking for sixty five miles they were going to make us walk across sand to cross this godforsaken event off our to-do lists. My heart sank into my crappy shoes and I allowed myself to sit down until it was time to cross the threshold.

And that was my complete undoing.

Forty five minutes later when they announced that it was time to finish what we'd started, I couldn't move. I tried to stand up and my rubbery legs collapsed underneath me. I summoned every ounce of strength I could muster and willed my limbs to stand up but I fell again. I couldn't even stand up.

I could not believe it. After all that, I was done, mere meters from my goal. I had never experienced such a feeling of disappointment in myself; I had pushed myself beyond all my reasonable limits but I had not imagined that I physically wouldn't be able to tread every step.

Suddenly I felt my body rising up off the ground and looked up to see that I had been flanked by two women who looked to be about forty years my senior. They threw my arms around their shoulders and, their arms linked around my waist, dragged my sorry ass across the sand and over the finish line.

Despite my acute embarrassment that these women probably had grandchildren there to watch them finish this thing and they were pulling *me* along, I couldn't thank these two ladies enough.

It was done. I had survived. My husband and my friend for whom I had dedicated myself to this event were there to greet me at the finish line. My physical therapist boyfriend came over to say farewell. He handed me a huge pink gerbera daisy.

"Congrats!" he said and gave me a big bear hug. "You did great!"

"Thanks for all your help!" I said, "You saved the day!"

"It was my pleasure," he said kindly. "See you next year!"

Haha, right.

My husband tried to pick me up to carry me to the car but it hurt so much I made him put me down.

There was much hobbling over the next few days, followed by an excruciating bout of plantar fasciitis. My husband actually did have to pick me up to get me in and out of the shower as I literally couldn't lift my legs high enough to clear the edge of the bathtub. It took me a while to be able to climb stairs again without grimacing.

But. All that said, I DID it, and it was for a great cause.

On your left, breast cancer!

DREAMING OF SLEEP

Alex is a "terrible" sleeper, and at age three and a half, is still up several times during the night, every night. This was a total shock to my husband's and my smug parenting sensibilities.

The first time around, we were *those* parents; the ones whose baby slept through the night at eight weeks and, barring the odd night terror here or illness there, has been sleeping like a champ ever since. It never occurred to us that our second baby wouldn't exhibit this endearing quality and replicate his sisters textbook sleeping patterns at the same tender age, so it blindsided us like a freight train when it became clear the dark circles were going to become permanent fixtures beneath our bloodshot eyes.

I should also mention that I am not a person who reads parenting books. As I so rapidly discovered, if as few as two children from the same parents can be so different in almost every way, it doesn't ring true to me that anyone can capture the secret method to overcoming a particular parenting hurdle that will work for all children. You must put your baby to sleep at exactly six o'clock every night… you must bounce the baby on your right knee at exactly a forty-five degree angle for ten minutes while making a shushing noise… you must let the baby cry it out and within three nights they will sleep for fourteen continuous hours… you must allow your baby to cry for five minutes before you go in the first time, and then eleven minutes the second time and then seventeen minutes the third time and make sure not to talk to them, pick them up, make eye contact with them or acknowledge their tearful, sorrowful little faces in any way, shape or form…

With all due respect to the experts, and lord knows, they have seen many more children than I, in my very unprofessional opinion, you have to use your own intuition and instincts in this parenting gig and trust that you will be able to figure out what works for you and your own child.

In an act of desperation I once succumbed to the cry it out theory, only to discover a nasty side effect to this method of sleep training. It appears that when my son cries for an extended period of time, he becomes so snotty and so distraught that he throws up. Our pediatrician did warn us that sometimes this happens when kids get really worked up. And, it's all very well and good for those who've had a full eight hours of continuous sleep to say *then let them throw up.*

However, as the mother of the child in this state, instead of just losing the fifteen minutes it would have taken to get him back to sleep had I gone in there when I first heard him crying, now I had to change Alex's sheets, clean him up, change him from head to toe, calm him back down and then still get him back to sleep. Not to mention the terrible tugging at my maternal heartstrings; it distresses me so badly to hear a baby crying that in public it's all I can do to keep myself from running over there, pulling the child out of its mothers arms and trying to console it myself. And here the mother is me, and the power to comfort my child is mine. So I do.

Night after night after week after month of sleep deprivation can start to do funny things to a person. All is fair in love and sleep and sometimes you do whatever it takes when it's three in the morning and you have to get up for work in two and a half hours. It reached the point when, around the third or fourth interruption to our REM sleep cycles, my husband and I would often wind up putting Alex in our bed.

Yes, I know in western society this is considered a total, unforgivable abomination. Yet every time we did, Alex would finally sleep like the proverbial baby, his cuddly body curled up next to me, his little pudgy feet prodding my husband in the back all night long.

One particular night, he had been wailing in his crib for a good while and I finally stumbled out of bed to go get him. He was standing in his crib, leaning against the railing nearest to the door and even in the dimmed nightlight I could see how blotchy his face was. His eyes were swollen from crying and there were tears in his hairline and even in his ears.

He reached his arms up to me and I pulled him out of the crib. He put his sodden head on my shoulder and I could feel the collar of his pajamas was wet with tears and sweat. He quieted instantly, and, without uttering a word myself, I walked back to my bedroom and laid him down on the pillow top between Russell and me. I climbed in next to him, up against the edge of the queen sized bed to give the three of us enough room.

His eyes were already closed and he reached out and placed his soft, chubby palms on both of my cheeks. He pulled my head close to his until our foreheads were touching and tenderly rubbed my face. "Mommy," he murmured, and exhaled deeply. Then he was out like a light and we didn't hear a peep out of him until the morning.

When he slept in our bed, we realized that part of the issue was Alex's restlessness. He would thrash and throw himself around like he was wrestling a team of dream state alligators.

The second factor was the matter of his "supersonic" hearing.

When he was born, my son failed his hearing test. Twice. Following the initial upheaval of TTN that set in within several hours after Alex was born, I chalked the failure of the first test up to the trauma of not being able to breathe on his own, and the four subsequent days he spent on oxygen, fighting for his life. In those first few days he was too exhausted from the effort of simply breathing to keep his eyes open for any length of time, let alone react to the noise and stimuli around him.

The hospital did a retest on the day we were going home, and to my dismay, Alex failed it again. My own paternal grandparents were deaf and led full, productive lives so I knew this wasn't insurmountable in any way. It was just a wrinkle we weren't anticipating, and would mean an adjustment to our family's way of life.

We were referred to a pediatric audiologist and my son was scheduled for his third hearing test. When we arrived at the doctor's office at the appointed time on the appointed day, Alex was fast asleep. My heart sank again; I thought they would turn us away and that we would have to come back yet another day to know for sure whether or not our son could hear.

It turns out hearing can be determined using brainwaves' reaction to sound, so they attached electrodes to Alex's head and my son slept soundly for the duration of the examination.

Just minutes after the test was completed, we got the diagnosis. Not only could Alex hear, the technician jokingly gave us a word of warning. "Watch out," she laughed, "He has 'supersonic' hearing in his left ear!"

Prophetic words, if she only knew.

I would painstakingly rock him for thirty to forty minutes, his head on my left shoulder, his arms tucked in between his tummy and mine, his binky squeaking more and more slowly until he finally gave in and nodded off. I would keep up the rocking until I felt him get heavier and knew he was really asleep.

The next phase was a delicate and risky operation. With drop side cribs now a thing of the past and my short arms no match for the lowest mattress setting, there was always the clumsy freefall as I tried to transfer him into the crib. About half the time that was all it took to send us back to the drawing board, but sometimes, I would actually get him to make contact with the sheet without waking him up.

Then, as I turned to leave the room, my knee or ankle would crack and rather than just open his eyes and sniffle, Alex would leap up in bed, and, clinging to the crib railing more than half asleep, shriek like an inconsolable banshee. And we'd kiss the last hour of effort goodbye.

Next we tried music. I put a CD player in Alex's room and brought in my arsenal of comforting collections of lullabies, some with singing and some just instrumental. The songs were soothing enough to get Alex to drift off fairly easily but the change in volume between one song ending and the other beginning kept waking him up.

The fan was our next move. We pinned a lot of hopes on this piece of plastic as we put it in his room the first night. Of course in order to drown out other noise it had to be on the arctic gust setting that nearly blasted me out the room when I first turned it on. We got a few decent weeks out of the fan but then Alex acclimated to that too and eventually, being on all night, the motor began to give out. The uneven whirring of the blades weren't enough to keep him in lala-land and we had struck out again.

I was desperate in a way that I had never been before. I am not a prima donna about my sleep and I knew the job was dangerous when I took it but I was at the end of my rope. Unfortunately there was really nothing that helped and we just had to ride it out. Three out of the four members of our family were in a constant state of grumpiness.

We did finally reach a stage where Alex would only wake up once or twice in a night. To us that began to feel like a full night's sleep. But then something would happen or he would hit a new developmental phase and our rhythm would be thrown off again. Like the train, for instance, the tracks for which we didn't even know were located so close to our neighborhood when we bought our house until our son's sensitive hearing brought it to our attention.

Yet every night, several times a night, it was directly to blame for the demise of our date with the Sandman. At various ungodly intervals such as eleven at night or three in the morning, the sadistic train driver would tear through our quiet suburban haven and ferociously clang the bell again and again and again until I heard the familiar shrieking down the hall. I would wearily drag myself out of bed and go into Alex's room to find him standing at the crib rails like a tiny jailbird, furiously rubbing his eyes. It got to the point that any time he woke up, Alex would mumble, "Tain wake up me."

It really was loud, and it seemed to get increasingly worse. I can certainly understand the need for a train whistle to warn people to get out of the way, and having been on board a train that once hit a person in a parked car on the tracks, I know firsthand that this is no joke. However at three in the morning this continuous ringing just sounded a little excessive.

Then one day I received a promotional flyer in the mail. Somewhere near the middle of the booklet was a very true to life red corvette with lifelike stickers and working headlights that just so happened to be a toddler bed. And this remarkably realistic and completely amazing bed just happened to be on sale. I didn't even hesitate. My husband and I agreed that Alex would go gaga over this item and we purchased it the day it went on sale.

When we introduced Alex to his new bed it was love at first sight. He was completely smitten and bubbling with excitement. We bought it to coincide with a move to our new house and were hoping it would help him transition to a big boy bed while also easing the upheaval of his new surroundings.

There were stars in Alex's eyes as he climbed into bed for his first night in his new room. We showed him how to switch on the headlights and he literally squealed with delight.

However, when it became clear that we intended for him to actually stay in his new bedmobile for the whole night, things derailed rather rapidly.

Alas, the only person who spent any quality time sleeping in the big car bed was me. I would lie down in the bed to try to coax Alex to follow suit but invariably, I would knock out after two minutes. When I would finally wake up at around three o'clock in the morning, it took some pretty impressive acrobatics to practically levitate out of his bed and creep out of the room like a ninja lest the sound of the mere effort it took to do this would wake him up. It wouldn't be another five minutes before we heard the familiar cries and a curly mop would materialize next to my side of the bed. Now that there weren't any bars to keep him contained within his bed there was no stopping him.

Sometimes we wouldn't even wake up; it was only upon finding one of our backs or shoulders had become a percussion instrument and the kicking finally caused us to open our eyes that we realized he had wriggled into our bed at some point during the night.

On one particular occasion I woke up because I

felt water dripping into my eye. I opened the rapidly blinking eyelid and discovered that after I had fallen asleep, Alex had snuck out of the room, gone to retrieve all the dinosaurs he'd bathed with that evening that had been left in the tub to dry off, and was staging a very soggy reenactment of Jurassic Park on my pillow.

Another time I woke up in the middle of the night to find I had been covered from head to toe in tissues, lovingly and carefully quilted on and around me. I looked over and found my boy with the empty tissue box, beaming at me with pure love in his eyes and a sweet, serene smile. "I thought you looked cold, Mommy," he confessed. "So I wrapped you in tissues to keep you warm!" I couldn't help but smile back at the sweet thought and effort it must have taken to do this. So instead of picking him out for mummifying me at midnight I kissed his soft dewy cheek and thanked him for looking after me. And then told him it was very, very, very late and he needed to go to sleep.

There was one more gimmick I was willing to try. Perhaps a few minutes of calming yoga before bed could do the trick. I announced the new addition to our routine, and both kids were more than up for the task. We gathered on the floor of my bedroom and I explained that we'd do a few minutes of yoga before story time every night, and that we'd rotate who got to lead the session. I of course was the leader the first night, and took the kids through some basic poses.

The second night, Alex wanted to be the leader, and instead of doing a couple of calming stretches we tromped around like BIIIIIG DADDY GOWIWWAS and snarled and pounced at each other like leopards. The third night, when Mia told Alex it was her turn to be the captain, he burst into tears because he wanted "Mommy to be the pirate again." By the fourth night, in direct contrast to its well-intentioned reason for being added to the bedtime starting lineup, yoga had proved to be successful only in whipping my children into a complete wild frenzied circus of excitement. Thus, our newly adopted ritual also fell victim to the nocturnal household chopping block.

So there it was. We guiltily continued to let Alex sleep in our bed; it was more important that he start actually making it through a whole night without waking up than where this took place. When he was finally old enough to really articulate it, he told me he couldn't sleep because he was afraid to be alone. He wasn't scared of monsters under the closet or of the dark. He was simply afraid of being alone.

And while society goes through its phases of dictating how we should raise our children as of that day or decade, children, who are oblivious to what is considered right or wrong, don't fall into a one size fits all parenting model. They just are who they are and need what they need, even if those needs are not the same as their friends at daycare or the kid next door or even their siblings in the room next door.

I couldn't shake the instinctive feeling that maybe

us Westerners have this sleeping thing all wrong. Recently, upon a quarter past wee hour in the morning, berating myself for being a terrible failure as a mother because my son won't sleep through the night and in his own bed, I googled children's sleeping customs around the world. I was relieved and vindicated to find out that in almost all societies besides the West, babies and children sleep in their parents' beds or at least rooms, across the globe.

So, I kind of just threw in the towel about the whole sleep thing. Every so often I will hear another parent bare their soul and admit that their seven year old still sleeps in the bed with them, or that they also fall asleep in their kids' beds because they just have to get some shuteye and it's come to that.

I know my son won't be eighteen years old and still sleeping in my bed, so I'm going to wait for him to ride out this phase as he eventually will. Then I'll probably still be up all night, still not sleeping, wondering where he is at three in the morning and who he's out with, and longing for those sweet, early days when we used to snuggle next to each other in the big car bed.

WRITING CELEBRATION

It's a tradeoff, this mothering business. My friends who are stay at home moms wish they had a job to go to, or some time to themselves; time to just exist in their brains and string a thought together without being interrupted to the point that they forgot what they were even trying to work out.

Some of them feel trapped, spending all day in the company of small people who constantly need their time and attention, with all the sweet and volatile moments that come with it, finding they haven't had an adult conversation, or at least one that didn't involve the bathroom and the various functions accomplished within, in a long time. Some feel unappreciated and taken for granted; there is no paid time off bank for moms, there are no comp days or temps who can fill in. This is a hardcore, 24/7 commitment, and quitting is not an option.

On the other side of the pendulum swing is the likes of me, the working moms who drop off our children every morning at daycare or, if we're lucky, relatives, in exchange for a heaping serving of guilt and the occasional tear to wipe away as we drive off in our quiet cars to our occupations. These are the moms who toil the day away in the relative solitude so craved by the stay at home moms, wondering each minute how our children are doing, if they've taken that first step without us there to witness it, if they've uttered that first word without us there to hear it, if they're even giving us a thought as they get infinitesimally older on the playground each afternoon.

Society likes to make itself feel better by saying that it was my choice to go back to work and put my career in front of my duties as a mother. But the fact is the choice is not mine to make. I have to part with my kids every day so I can have the financial wherewithal to provide for them, and it's no small cut of my paycheck either. Why do it you ask? Because for me, it's not a wash. I earn just enough for us to depend too heavily on my salary to quit. Since the net is still more than the monthly daycare expense, it doesn't make monetary sense to do so.

As a mother in this latter category, it is all I would give to be able to spend the day with my children in unhurried time, devoting my attention to them instead of a sea of unread e-mails and excel spreadsheets. Unfortunately being a working mom means getting caught somewhere in the limbo between these two divisions of motherhood. I am still on the hook for the before school breakfast-getting-ready-making-lunch morning routine, and the dinner-homework-bath-bed evening routine in addition to working full time. Not only do my children miss out on me during the typical working hours, they don't have my full attention in the mornings either, as the demands of my job require me to be on conference calls as early as five thirty AM and it all overlaps. Most days are a continuous meeting marathon and I don't have time to grab lunch, never mind step away for an hour or two.

When I find all the notes in Mia's backpack asking parents to volunteer or show up for various activities during school hours, I automatically dismiss them, knowing I can't get away to attend since they are scheduled during work hours. In fact Mia had stopped even asking me to go to these events as the answer was always "I'm so sorry love, I have to work."

I had been managing a two year initiative at work. It was an exhilarating opportunity at first, and opened many doors as I learned volumes about a new business segment and had the good fortune to work with a slew of very competent and dedicated team members. Yet the seventy hour work weeks began to take their toll. When I finally ended up wearing a holter monitor for forty eight hours to track the heart palpitations that hadn't slowed down in over four days, I realized that as noble as it was to spend every waking moment (and too many of the ones when I should have been sleeping) slaving over this project, I was literally going to drive myself into the ground from the stress.

I also came to the sobering realization that if I did actually work myself into the grave over this project, the company would still go on without missing a beat. I kept telling my family that there is nothing in the world more important to me than they are, yet I was putting work first for fourteen hours a day. The other ugly fact is that in an economy where layoffs loom ever large in the background like a foreboding reminder that if you're not willing to put in the time, someone else will, it's hard to set boundaries and just log out after your eight hours for the day.

The project finally started winding down to a close and my boss dropped the bomb that he was leaving the company. With the workforce reduction going off all around us like landmines, I intuitively knew this would happen but it was still a shock. He was a great boss, one of those people who gave his staff trust and autonomy and empowered us to make decisions. He had our backs and we had his; I was really sad to see him go.

When he left I stepped into his role on another huge project and essentially went from the frying pan into the fire. I will lose over a hundred hours of time off this year because, due to the oppressively urgent deadlines of one project or another, cannot take time off. What few days I did take here and there were spent with half an eye on my work phone anyway, checking in to the work e-mails that couldn't wait a day for my response due to their dire urgency and severe deadlines.

And I realized that there was always going to be a reason why I couldn't take time off. There will always be another project, another urgent e-mail, another escalated "fire" or hysterical customer who needs my help immediately. There will never be a good time to take a breather. So I will need to just take one anyway.

That is how it was that when I opened Mia's backpack one random Thursday and saw a yellow slip of paper inviting me to the second grade writing celebration, it made me stop and smell the proverbial roses. I had missed out on two years of field trips, intramural sports events and classroom volunteer time. I was going to the writing celebration.

My new boss was very understanding about my request to take a little time out the next Tuesday. I shoved this second serving of guilt about leaving for a few hours aside, reminding myself that in fact, having started my day at five thirty AM and taking no breaks, leaving at one thirty was a full eight hour day anyway.

I got to Mia's school a little early and had time to find a good seat in the classroom where the event was being held. I shut off the ringer on my phone and put it into my purse. I didn't want to be on the phone, responding to the crisis of the hour, when Mia came in. I wanted to give her my undivided attention. The volunteer moms were setting up snacks and drinks on tables in the back of the room and I bit back the pang of envy.

After about ten more minutes, the children started filing in. I saw Mia. She hadn't taken off her woolen hat from when she left the house in the morning, and I was struck by her face; she looked unenthused and sad. Mia is now getting to the preteen stage. Of course I had known it would come one day, the sassiness and moodiness, telling me how much I embarrassed her and that she wasn't my little baby anymore. I just didn't know it would come as soon as the end of her seventh year, so it tugged at my heart even more to see her face so down and beyond her years.

As she walked past the chairs to find her seat on the mat at the front of the classroom, Mia turned her head towards the audience and scanned the crowd. Her eyes met mine and her whole face lit up as she broke out in a gigantic grin.

"MOMMY!" she yelped and broke out of line to come over to me. She was intercepted by one of the kindergarteners whom she gracefully hugged and then pointed at me. "My mom's here!"

She ran over to me and threw her arms around me as she jumped into my lap. "You're here, Mom!" she sang.

"Of course, love! I wouldn't have missed it," I grinned back at her, squeezing her just as tightly. We beamed at each other and then I snuck in a quick kiss on her head before she had to go and sit back down. The hum of the crowd began to hush as the teachers got the event underway. Some of the children would be reading stories they'd written in class. Not everyone would get to read in front of the audience but there would be smaller groups afterwards where all the kids could share their efforts. Every so often, Mia turned around to look at me as if to check that I was really truly there and we smiled at each other, the light in her eyes dazzling me and putting a lump in my throat.

Yes, the e-mails were piling up in my inbox. The instant messages were popping up on my laptop back in its docking station on my desk. The voice messages were undoubtedly streaming into my voicemail box as well. But I had made my daughter feel important and the look on her face was proof that I had done the right thing. For the first time in a long time, I was exactly where I needed to be. I really *wouldn't* have missed it for the world.

UNASPIRIN

After you've had more than a few spins around the sun you start to get to know yourself pretty well. For instance, I know that I study better with music on in the background, that I prefer dancing to running, that I get tired every afternoon around three o'clock. I know that my tea just tastes better with milk in it, that I feel alive in the sunshine, that I have absolutely no tolerance for medication or substances of any kind. None. In fact, when I get sick, I will take the path of homeopathic resistance, switching to traditional medicine only if the cold or flu at hand is so severe that I have no other choice. And even then, I take the children's dose of children's cold meds and it does the trick perfectly.

The summer after I graduated from college, I had my wisdom teeth taken out. During my pre-op visit the nurse had insisted I take two valium home with me, to be taken on the morning of the surgery to help me relax. I was more than a little dubious about the valium and assured her I was fine with the thought of them cutting four impacted molars out of my jaws without it. Again she insisted they would only help take the edge off and to take them in the morning.

On the morning of the big day, being too young to trust my instinct which was protesting rather loudly, I took one of the said edge removing pills. My husband and I were dating at the time, and he fortunately had volunteered to drive me there that day, because I was so gone by the time we were ready to leave the house he had to pick me up and carry me out to the car. I have no recollection of the drive over there, although I do vaguely remember him scooping me out of the front seat and carrying me into the oral surgeon's rooms, and carrying me back out to the car when it was all over.

My friends have literally bought me rounds of beer in shot glasses and tease me about the thimbleful of rum that awaits me after a particularly long, hard day at work.

So when I found myself standing in front of the medicine cabinet in the break room at work, I really should have known better.

I'd had a visit to the dermatologist the day before and she had cut out several moles and freckles for biopsy. The incision sites and stitches were a little uncomfortable and I was told I could take Tylenol for the pain but not to have aspirin as it can cause bleeding.

When I arrived at work that morning I got swept into the routine meeting frenzy and when the pain started getting noticeable around noon, I figured I'd take my Tylenol.

Looking around in my bag I realized I had forgotten to pack that convenient little bottle. I asked around to see if anyone else had some in their handbags but in the brave new world of political office correctness, it was now against policy to give out medication to anyone else.

Somewhere in the recesses of my mind I remembered seeing a first aid kit mounted to the wall in the break room. I made my way into the kitchenette and opened the Pandora's box of minor scrapes and bruises self-help. There was quite a collection in there! Eye wash, scissors, gauze, burn cream in little packets, alcohol wipes, band aids in every size and shape. And, a little assortment of different pain pills.

Being generic, I expected to see descriptions like "acetaminophen" and "ibuprofen." Yet for some strange reason there were neither of those. Instead, what appeared to be the safest bet was the "unaspirin" baggie containing two tablets of the same. I opened the little paper pouch and for another inexplicable reason, popped both capsules into my mouth. I washed them down with a few swigs of water and returned to my desk.

I was up to my eyebrows in a business area requirements document review. Twenty eight pages of acronyms and how they interact is tedious at the best of times, but I started having severe trouble focusing. I blinked furiously and even shut my eyes a few times, but it seemed to be getting progressively worse. Finally I pushed myself back in my chair and looked away from the screen.

Everything slowed down and had become really quiet. My every movement was really exaggerated and strange, like someone had hit the pause button and was letting me move a muscle every few seconds in slow motion.

And as I sat there, the sensation of floating becoming more and more pronounced, I suddenly realized what was going on.

I was high. High off a two pack of unaspirins from the office medicine cabinet.

In my haze I sluggishly recalled that, for the first time in my life, I had forgotten to eat breakfast that morning. The two five hundred milligram happy tabs of unaspirin on an empty stomach proved to be my ticket to Puff the Magic Dragon's corporate lair.

Somewhere deep inside my latent rational conscience, I knew I couldn't sign off on these requirements in this state. I had to tell my boss why I wouldn't be turning in my tome of tedium by that afternoon.

I stood up and felt like a helium balloon that had just been cut from its string. I gradually wafted down the hall and into my boss's office. My then boss also happens to be a good friend of mine and spun around when she saw me hovering in the doorway.

"Hey Romi!" she smiled.

"Hiiiiiiiii," I grinned back and waved at her in a large exaggerated fan.

She squinted at me, curious. "Um, Romes, are you okay?"

"Uh huuuuuuh," I replied. And just stood there smiling at her, about two feet off the ground in her doorway.

"Why don't you come in and sit down?" she offered.

"Okay," I said and did my best to slide down into the chair on the opposite side of her desk. "I... ate some... unaspirins..." I began. "In the... break. Room."

The situation registered on my boss's face. She knows me well and couldn't hide her amusement. "How many did you take?" she asked.

"Ummmmmm...." I started. "Two. I think... I'm... hiiiiiiigh." I grinned at her. I did have to admit that I was feeling no pain. In fact I was feeling nothing at all. "I have... to go... to. A. Meeting...about the..."

"Please don't make any decisions this afternoon," she cut in, joking. And then more seriously, "I think you need to go home, Romes."

I was about to insist that I could handle it but really, I was ten sheets to the wind. "Yuuuuup," I agreed. My boss escorted me back to my desk and explained to my two immediate team mates what was going on. Also good friends of mine, they thought this was completely hilarious, and good naturedly agreed to drive me home. Katrina drove my car while Melissa dropped me off in hers.

Naturally, they laughed at me all the way there and I was the brunt of many jokes for a good long while afterwards.

After I floated into the house I made myself something to eat, thinking I could somehow sop it up with a sandwich like I did in college when I was drunk but it was no use. I couldn't get my head straight no matter what I tried and finally just had to sleep it off.

It wasn't too terribly surprising that not long after this curious little incident, all traces of pain pills disappeared from the work break room medicine box, unaspirin and otherwise.

I did feel bad for every subsequent unsuspecting headache sufferer who went to the box of ailment relief only to walk away with their heads still throbbing due to the fact that I have the tolerance of a gnat. It was like being the kid whose act of defiance earns the whole class an after school detention.

But that was crying over spilled milk. The glory days of free unaspirin were over as soon as they started. Apparently getting high in the workplace, even if induced embarrassingly from medicine cabinet loot and not from something more impressive, is a no-no. Luckily for me, there is now a handy bottle of children's Tylenol in my bag at all times in case my kids should need it. So if the need for some impromptu pain relief ever presents itself again, this time I should be all set.

HOW TO HAVE A PLAYDATE

Once I got married, I thought my dating days were over. My husband and I have often discussed the fact that we don't believe in "the one" – it doesn't seem possible that in a world of seven billion people there could be only *one* pre-destined soul with whom you might find that perfectly-suited forever bliss.

Russell and I simply got each other, found the same things funny, and no matter how much time we spent together, we still wanted to get up the next morning and see each other again. As Russell so gingerly puts it, "You're the only person I can actually stand to be around day after day." It may not be the stuff of romance novels, but twenty four years later it's nothing to sniff at, and for us is as real and good as it gets.

And then came children. Now, it turned out, not only did both my husband and I have to like the other couple, but our kid and theirs had to gel as well, and then once we had more than one child, the siblings needed to get along on top of that.

It's a very complicated dance of chemistry and coordination to appease the friendship Cupid in just the right way, and to find others who think your children are the best thing since sliced bread, almost as much as you do.

Yet somehow, those rare finds do sift through all the various layers of matchmaking requirements and a sparkling new acquaintanceship is born.

Just like dating, the beginning is a fun and exciting time, a period where you discover all the weird and wonderful things that made you like this family so much to begin with. You realize just how much you have in common. Petunia ALSO loves to eat her cereal with a fork! Johnny is completely besotted with dinosaurs too! Fred also wakes up twenty times every night! Cannon Beach is our favorite as well! I *LOVE* dulce la leche!

And after the few awkward meetings at a play center or coffee shop or local children's museum, it's time to take this new relationship to the next logical stage: the play date at home. Sometimes the other parent will initiate this bold move, or sometimes you ask about it yourself, heart pounding in case they say no, but would they want to come over and play at your house?

Then finally after all the logistics like exchanging addresses, confirming whether or not any of the children have food allergies, taking nap schedules into consideration and checking calendars for the next month or two, the stage is set for the big day.

Now perhaps this next part isn't as big a deal for other moms as it is for me, perhaps other organized moms who aren't operating on three hours of sleep and can actually string a coherent thought together might not find this to be such an ordeal. But for me, the preparation for the play date is nothing short of the sort of effort other people put into a wedding or graduation or maybe the sale of their house or a NASA launch.

This is because, due to the scurry and bustle of everyday life, and despite my best attempts to prove otherwise, my house is usually in a state of total disarray. Read: complete disaster. Of course, we don't want to scare off our new friends before we've even gone through a whole afternoon with them. Therefore after the invitation has been extended and accepted, Operation Slum Reversal is deployed immediately.

The tiny obstacle, naturally, is that when you have small children, Operation Slum Reversal is executed simultaneously with Operation Continue to Ensure the House Looks like a Pigsty, the results of which just turn out to be a monumental waste of time. However, you can't not ever reciprocate a play date because your house is a mess; that simply isn't a good enough reason, and certainly won't go very far in assisting your burgeoning alliance to grow.

Besides which, one should theoretically have ones house in such a state that you can actually see the floor, with or without the incentive of someone else coming over to see it. So, without any further ado, allow me to let you in on such an occasion.

The mother of your child's friend asks if you would like to have a play date.

Yes, of course you would!

The other mom offers graciously to have you all over at her house.

You won't hear of it! It would be your pleasure to have them over. Because it really would. And, because you are a lunatic with a secret bent for self-torture.

Great!

You suggest the Saturday after next.

She checks her iPhone and counters with Sunday.

Hmm, you vaguely recall that there is something going on that day but cannot remember what it actually is. You suggest the weekend after that.

Saturday works for them! Their child naps between noon and two in the afternoon.

Your child only naps in the car on the way to play dates or parties, or when you desperately need to go to the store to pick something up at some random point in the day, or ten minutes before dinner is ready. Agree that two thirty is perfect.

In the three weeks between arranging the play date and the morning thereof, make somewhere between five and seventeen attempts to get the house to the point where you can consider opening the front door to anyone but your immediate family.

However, you can't live in a museum and it's just not happening.

The night before the soiree, when your house still looks like a herd of goats tore through it earlier that day, set your alarm for seven in the morning.

Your children wake you up at six thirty.

Get the coffee started.

Sit down with both the kids and explain that unfortunately it's going to be a bit of a humdrum morning because you have to clean like a crazy person and won't be able to play with them right now. AND, they cannot make a mess, they need to help put their toys away. Remind them that they will be able to have a fabulous time with their friends and play all afternoon so the payoff will be worth the initial boredom.

Both children smile and nod.

Smile back at your cherubs.

Throw back a cup or four of coffee and give the kids breakfast.

Pick up a sponge and start cleaning with a vengeance.

After about twenty minutes, realize your children are watching TV and the floor is still littered with toys.

Ask your children to pack their toys away.

Get out the vacuum cleaner and begin sucking up all the dust, paper shreds, feather wisps from toy boas, tiny pieces of Lego, several Polly Pocket outfits and random socks. Oops. But really, they should have been picked up by their respective owners during aforementioned attempts five through seventeen.

Empty the vacuum and restore it to the closet.

Pop back into the den. Older child is sprawled on the floor, drawing. Approximately half a ream of paper is strewn all about on the carpet, and there are copious amounts of pens and colored pencils on the floor. Toddler has flung all the throw pillows onto the floor, removed all the cushions from the couch and tossed those in front of the fireplace, and is jumping on the springs of the couch, clad in only a diaper that is sagging down his butt.

Kneel down in front of older child. Praise her for her really amazingly lifelike drawing of a cat family, and remind her that she can draw anything she wants after her friend arrives, but it's now time to put all that stuff away, upstairs, in her room, which still looks like a minefield. (Stare at the cat picture for a while though, it really is incredible.)

She assures you that she will pack it all away.

Go over to toddler and scoop him up, mid bounce. He shrieks with laughter and wriggles wildly to get out of your arms. Hold him gently but firmly and remind him that his friends are coming over, so we need to put all the cushions and pillows back on the couch and get dressed.

Toddlers face clouds over and he explains that he can't do that.

Assure him that he really can, and tell him you're

going to have a race and see how quickly he can do it.

Toddler's bottom lip juts out and he hangs his head down. He reiterates his inability to clean up, in a small, dejected voice.

Older child steps in to the rescue and starts picking up the toys, calling out that she's winning the race.

Toddler freaks out and crumples into a sobbing heap in the corner.

In between the racking sobs, express to your toddler the need to pick up the toys.

Begin wiping down the countertops.

Suddenly notice all the spills and sticky handprints on the cabinet doors. Scrub those off furiously.

Scrub the microwave inside and out, and then the fridge handles and little water tray under the icemaker.

Mop the floor.

Go check on the laundry, having washed the few non-sweatpants items that your children agree to wear on play dates without too much of a fight.

Discover you have laundered a disposable diaper that your son must have put into the hamper; its gelatinous remnants all over the clean, freshly spun clothes like squishy confetti.

Start rinse cycle as you cannot possibly pick off all the little blobs.

Give children lunch so they will be fed and happy when their guests arrive.

Toddler doesn't want to eat. But he drinks three cups of milk so decide not to fight that fight today.

Jump in the shower while the kids are eating (or not eating, respectively) and then throw on your own clothes.

It is now almost two o'clock. The home stretch. This is the part where you notice all the dust on the TV and TV stand, dirt on the windows, and all other things that need your attention but can't possibly be done in thirty minutes.

You nearly have a heart attack when the doorbell rings, thinking your guests have arrived early.

Run to the door to see your toddler, who has opened the front door, with his finger on the doorbell.

Exhale. Ask the toddler to come back into the house.

Toddler rings the doorbell four thousand, two hundred and ninety five more times and then comes back inside.

Tell the kids to go and get dressed.

Frantically dust the living room, do your best with the windows and mirrors, and clean the bathrooms.

Find a counter that you missed and grab a garbage bag. Do a one armed sweep and just pull everything off the counter into the bag.

Throw the bag into the garage.

Arrange the pillows on the couch so that they cover some of the stains from cranberry juice spills, goldfish crumbs that have been mashed onto one of the seats, and a million dried tears that had picked up chocolate, fruit and other snacks along their descent down little chins.

Fling yourself onto the couch and sit still long enough to let your heart rate return to normal.

Approximately two minutes later the doorbell rings again.

Answer the door with a bright smile, hoping the flush of your cheeks, moderately matted hair and general sheen all over your skin doesn't give you away.

Friend and her children are relaxed and fresh-faced, nicely put together, and unlike yourself, not probably smelling slightly of moose.

Take your guests' jackets and shoes.

All the kids scamper upstairs to their bedrooms to play.

Ask the other mom if she'd like some tea, and offer standard blanket apology for the mess.

Of course, other mom has no idea that what has transpired in the eight hours prior to her arrival has virtually rendered the house a shrine in comparison, and the fact that she can actually see the carpet is proof enough that miracles do indeed still occur in our modern times.

Other mom assures you that she completely understands, and that her house is always a mess as well.

While that is probably not true and she is most

likely trying to spare your feelings, feel blissful and grateful for the reassurance. Relationship with other mom has suddenly been upgraded from acquaintance to good friend.

For the first time since six thirty that morning, really exhale and relax.

Make a mental note to try to keep the house looking like this so that the prep for next weekend's play date will be calm and enjoyable and less like a triathlon.

Really though, it will be wash, rinse and repeat. So, just put it out of your mind and bask in your nice cup of tea with your new best friend.

CHEW ON THIS

The pieces of sand dollar that I *did* manage to fish out of my boy's mouth had been crunched up into really small bits, so I figured he'd probably be fine. He'd suddenly become stone quiet; something that I used to look forward to hearing every once in a while, but since becoming a parent of a rambunctious boy, have learned to regard as VERY BAD.

I located him in the corner of the living room near a large indoor plant, chomping away on what sounded like a mouthful of rocks. Since having a mouthful of rocks is not something particularly foreign to my son, when he saw me coming, he quickly slid around the back side of the pot, wedging himself between the giant ceramic bowl and the corner of the room where the two walls meet. And there he frantically munched up the rest of the shell in his mouth double time as he knew I wasn't about to sit there and patiently wait for him to finish the rest of his marine skeleton hors d oeuvre in peace.

I dove behind the plant, which prompted him to

wriggle out the other side and make a run for the middle of the living room. I rapidly backed out and galloped after him, his tawny curls bouncing furiously as he lapped the coffee table. I tackled him into my arms and without a moment's hesitation, forced my forefinger into his mouth. Ignoring the teeth that were still attempting to gnash their victim, I swept my precarious digit back and forth trying in vain to get all the fragments out.

Unbelievable. How did it even taste good enough to eat?! All the hours I've slaved away making breakfast, lunch and dinner for my children and what finally made it down the gullet of the pickiest eater in the Pacific Northwest was a sand dollar?

"Yucky!" I frowned. "We don't eat things that are not food!"

"Uck!" he repeated, very proud of himself.

When I called the poison control center to double check this wasn't going to leave a mark, the woman on the line laughed at me and reassured me that sand dollars weren't going to hurt my boy, especially since the pieces were really small. "Just think of it as a calcium supplement," she said.

As we were winding down the call she said, "How old is he?"

"Sixteen months," I replied.

She chuckled and said, "Ah, yes. You may want to keep our number handy next to the phone."

Fantastic.

Eating dirt became a chronic issue at daycare.

Every evening I'd walk up to the little school house, wondering if Alex had heeded our little morning sermon before drop off. "We don't eat things that are not food, love," I'd say.

"Okay Mommy!" he'd reply sweetly, and give me a huge heart-melting grin.

Yet every day when he spied me, he'd literally drop what he was doing and come bounding over, yelling, "MOMMEEEEE!" As he threw his little arms around my neck and I scooped him up for a big hug, I'd feel the familiar scratch and then catch the remnants of sand-goatee all over his mouth and chin as he pulled away.

"Did you eat sand, sweetheart?" I'd ask.

"No," he'd lie, looking me right in the eye, the little gritty bits still fizzling on the surfaces of his molars as he spoke.

"Hmm, I think you did, love, I can see the sand on your face," I countered. Alternatively, I began to notice he'd run and hide and do a frantic sleeve licking session when I'd show up to get rid of the sand before I could see it.

When bark chips began to make their way into Alex's daily soil snack as well, I took him to the pediatrician. It turns out that Pica – eating things that are not food – is a real phenomenon and does affect some people. The biggest concern in this case is that Alex's iron levels might have been low but a quick test put those fears to rest. The doc just shrugged and said while it wasn't *his* first menu choice, there was nothing wrong with Alex and if anything, actually it would help build his immune system.

Oblivious to my mounting exasperation, Alex subsisted on a steady diet of bark chips and milk for many more moons.

One morning, in an attempt to stave off Alex's overwhelming desire to consume tiny pieces of wood for his mid-morning snack, I decided to make the kids homemade waffles for breakfast.

We had recently paid a visit to the local berry patch and had literally picked a bucket worth of blueberries that were now in the freezer. With the memory of the haul still fresh in his mind, Alex asked if we could add some in the batter.

I mulled this one over for a minute before responding. While of course like all mothers I usually seize any opportunity to get some fruit and veggies into my kids' mouths, I also know that Alex doesn't particularly enjoy blueberries.

"Do you like blueberries, love?" I asked him.

"Oh YES, Mommy!" he chirped brightly. "I DO wike them!"

I still wasn't convinced. "Will you actually eat a waffle if I add them?" I cross examined.

"Yes! I will, Mom!" he confirmed, nodding emphatically.

"Maybe you can put them on top afterwards?" I suggested, trying to reach a happy medium. That way if he changed his mind in the minute and a half it took to cook them, he could leave them off.

"No Mom! We have to put them *inside*," he insisted.

A little giddy with the thought that my child might actually have a halfway decent breakfast before school for once, I allowed myself to be conned into adding blueberries into the mixture.

While my kids played, I listened in to a conference call and blended all the ingredients. Soon the little blue fruits were sizzling and popping inside the hot waffle iron.

I cut the steaming pastries into strips and called the kids over to come sit down at the kitchen table.

"Waffles!" I sang.

"WAFFLES!" they shrieked in unison and bounded over to the table.

Mia sat down and took a big bite. "Mm, Mom, these are so scrummy," She grinned, "Thanks!"

"You're welcome! I'm so glad you like them!" I beamed back at her.

"These have purple in them!" Alex retorted, his nose wrinkled in disgust.

Here we go.

"Those are the blueberries that we talked about, love," I reminded him. "Remember? You wanted me to put them inside the waffles."

"But I don't wike bueberries!" he said. "I can't eat this bweakfast."

"Yes you can," I said. "I'm going to take them out." With that, I painstakingly picked out every solitary blueberry and handed Alex back the plate of waffle rubble.

He poked through the pile and located a miniscule crumb that still had a microscopic berry stain on it.

"There's still purple!" he cried triumphantly, pushing the plate away. "YUCK!"

"You know what?" I said, calling in my trump card, "You need to have a no thank you bite." No thank you bites are what his daycare teachers insist the children eat before they are allowed to say they don't like a food. They have to try at least one mouthful.

Alex knew he'd been played but he did take the crumb and gingerly tasted it. His eyes widened in surprise.

"I DO wike it, Mommy! I wike the bueberries!" he gushed, and helped himself to a bigger morsel. "Now please can you put them all back inside?"

Sigh.

I should have just stuck with the bark chips.

MINNESOGA

In the calm bliss that is my home office, I don't have to worry about bad hair days or whether or not my shoes match my outfit or about the dress code in general. While my husband probably taxes the dark recesses of his mind every once in a while to remember what his wife looked like when she actually gave a damn about her appearance, or didn't have enough yoga pants to go ten days without having to launder them, I find this arrangement to be nothing short of perfection.

In our modern world of Webex, screen sharing and initiatives to stop corporate wasteful spending, I worked in this contented bubble for several years without so much as having to put on a pair of patent leather heels even once.

But, all good things come to an end, and thus I was summoned to an in-person meeting in Minnesota for a very important proposal my company was bidding.

The lead time from notice to attend and the start

of the session was ten days.

For a normal person, who adheres to a schedule of general physical upkeep, this would be something taken in stride. For me, for the obvious reasons stated above, this was the makeover version of defcon 1.

I have spent most of my life struggling with my weight. I always felt self-conscious about how I looked and in hindsight, the pictures prove that I wasn't really all *that* big. Before my wedding, I lost a copious amount of weight and finally stopped thinking of myself as fat. Sixteen years and two kids later, the pounds crept on insidiously, continuously, so now I have never looked worse but ironically I have never cared less. I just can't bring myself to muster up enough energy to feel badly about the way I look anymore.

While I have never been Barbie, there was once a time when I did elicit smiles from men who passed by me on the street. Of course this doesn't define me as a person or a woman, and most of my gender will probably condemn me for counting that as something worthy enough to even write about.

However, in my humble opinion, after you've popped out a few children and have generally gone to seed, the odd nod from someone who isn't legally bound to love you anyway to let you know that you aren't a complete write off is a nice feeling from time to time. So I knew I had officially crossed the line from pleasantly passably plump to plain old big when those smiles dried up and men stopped making eye contact with me. Nobody smiles at the fat lady. They don't even see her.

Losing the requisite sixty pounds in ten days was obviously not going to transpire. However, while I have worked with my peers and senior leadership for almost six years, at this point I had not yet met any of them face to face. I had to make some sort of effort, and put myself on an emergency diet to chip away as much as I could in the very small timeframe I had to work with.

The next and very serious item to conquer was the matter of child care. Both my husband's and my parents live thousands of miles away, and I couldn't ask my brother and sister in law who do live in town, and both work, to watch my children until eleven o'clock at night. My husband did a very fancy rescheduling effort at work and managed to change his Monday closing shift to day hours, and took Tuesday and Wednesday off. A friend of Mia's agreed to take her before and after school on Monday. We were all set for child care.

The following area requiring my attention was the matter of wardrobe. There simply wasn't anything hanging in my closet that was going to suffice. I had to drag my poor children off to the mall with me. I made myself promise that I would not stomp my feet, roar or swear. Or even huff. I perched my youngsters on the seat in the changing room and hung up the potential additions to my closet on a hook. Alex looked around, sizing up the cubicle.

"What is this place?" he asked innocently. "What are we doing in here?" It occurred to me just how long it had been since I'd gone on such a hunt.

"This is called a changing room, sweetheart," I said. "You try on clothes in here to see if you like them before you buy them."

"Oh," he said quietly, not quite getting it still, "Are we nearly done?" I wish, my love, I wish we were.

It was an uncharacteristically short shop. I reaped two sweaters and like a swarm of locusts that had exhausted their supply and had to move on, descended upon the next store and the next.

I am old enough to know that regardless of what hideous colors the fashion machine is churning out for the current season, I need to look for jewel tones or red. Wearing hot pink, cherry red or turquoise while my friends were clad in subtle forest green or ochre used to embarrass me as a child. I felt it drew too much attention to me and of course, was embarrassing simply because it wasn't "in." However, it is very freeing to be forty and not have to care about such things, so now I seek those colors out with no qualms. The teeny problem is that fashion is so uppity, not only does it force all the vomity lemon yellows, faded cornflower blues and pastel corals on us, it doesn't offer any choices from the normal palette as an alternative.

This made shopping, especially in my state of

procrastinated desperation, substantially more difficult. After a concerted weekend of efforts which nearly did all three of us in, I had found three sweaters, three camisoles, a wrap, two pairs of shoes and several pairs of pants.

Before I called it a day on our shopping challenge, there was one last item I had the presence of mind to look for. I needed a handbag that didn't have goldfish cracker remnants in it or pieces of petrified candy clinging to the zipper. This corporate approved bag needed to look like it hadn't lay on the hinges of a thousand changing tables or been the brunt of countless sippy cup tumbles.

I was losing my audience. My youngsters were done and quite frankly I was as well. I settled on a larger black one that had a removable shoulder strap and also handles. There were compartments, a good sign. This meant my usual bag fumbling might be kept to a minimum while digging around in there for various things.

One of my best friends who lives in Chicago immediately took on my case and promptly sent me two necklaces and a scarf, so the accessories were taken care of. She also provided round the clock real time advice on what matched with what, and what was appropriate versus a total no no. I love her. I am truly blessed to have friends like this.

Next on the agenda was a facial wax. This is one of the banes of my existence and had to be coordinated very carefully so that there was enough lead time to let my inflamed face calm down, and not enough time to turn back into Chewbacca before the meeting began. I had my brows and upper lip neatly deforested and to my detriment, allowed the beautician to talk me into applying hydrocortisone cream post-wax which promptly gave me a nestle crunch bar mustache and matching pocked unibrow where the fuzz had previously resided. Peachy.

My daily obsession with the scale confirmed that I was actually dropping weight! Not five pounds a day as I'd hoped, but it was at least heading in the right direction for a change.

I have run through airports more times than I care to remember. I am usually disorganized and always running late. This couldn't happen this time. I had a VERY narrow margin of time between landing and the start of the meeting day one kickoff: forty seven minutes to be exact. But I had a plan. This time, I really spent some energy on the mechanics of it.

I signed up for Hertz Gold so that my car would be ready and waiting for me when I arrived. I stuffed all my clothes, laptop and cosmetics into the required size bag so that I wouldn't have to check anything through and could just grab and go once we landed. I actually measured the bag according to the guidelines on the airline website and even upgraded myself to priority boarding so that I could get on first and *make sure* I could put my bag up in the overhead bin and not have to have my bag checked anyway if the flight was full.

A final glance at the scale the night before I left confirmed that I had indeed lost seven pounds. This kind of weight loss is unprecedented for me and I was pretty chuffed with myself. Ah, if only I'd started earlier.

I said goodnight to my babies and explained that it would be SUPER early when I left and I wasn't going to wake them up at four in the morning to say goodbye. I promised I'd call them each day to say good night and they promptly began to cry. I tried my best to reassure them that I would be back in no time, bearing presents, but they weren't having any of it. I wiped the tears off their sad faces and rubbed their backs until they finally fell asleep. Then I crawled into bed myself, satisfied that my bags were completely packed, boarding pass printed and everything waiting neatly by the front door.

The alarm was set for three thirty but I promptly sprang out of bed at three. I was out of the house by four, thirty minutes ahead of schedule. Excellent progress so far.

I made it to the airport with plenty of leeway, so had time to even go into the bathroom and carefully apply my makeup. I got my coffee, got to the terminal and waited. I spilled such a small amount of coffee on my sleeve that I didn't even count it as a spill.

Before long I was in the priority pack, making my way onto the plane. It took a while to get everyone on board. We were indeed overbooked so the bidding began to entice someone to take a later flight. It got to fifteen hundred dollars and I was dying to take it but I didn't have any wiggle room at all if I was going to get to Minneapolis on time.

Ten minutes before we were due to take off, the pilot came over the PA. "Ladies and Gentlemen," he began, "Normally I'd be welcoming you to flight 4279. But we are missing a critical part which is in Atlanta right now. We can't take off without it." Several of us began to laugh, myself included, waiting for him to say just kidding and we'd be on our way. "We'll need to deplane," he continued, "And we'll get you rerouted as soon as possible."

Are you freaking kidding me.

All that planning. All that planning and careful coordination to make it to my meeting on time and it had all gone to hell in fifteen seconds.

However. If there is a part missing from the plane, I don't particularly want to be on it, thirty five thousand feet up in the air.

It took about half an hour just to get off the plane and then another hour in line to get to the desk and begin negotiating for another flight. My only other option was to reroute through Los Angeles and get to Minneapolis marginally earlier than if I just waited the six hours for the rescheduled flight. I opted to wait.

Now I had six hours to kill. I called my boss to let him know what was going on, and then decided it was coffee time again. Although I was getting my high heeled sea legs back and no longer staggering around with a strut that was part chicken, part John Wayne, my toes were already numb and screaming at me. The shoes really had been comfy in the store for all of the two minutes I'd hmm'd and hah'd in them. Or maybe it had just been too long since I'd had to perch in a pair. I took them off and tromped across the airport, a shoe dangling from both my forefinger and middle finger, swinging next to my hip as I strode. I bee lined for a shoe store and bought a really cute and *truly* comfortable pair of black flats.

There was a musician set up just past the security entrance at the A, B, C gates. I curled up on a chair and listened to live piano music while I sipped my coffee and read a book. I can definitely think of worse ways to spend a work day.

I finally got to Minneapolis after six that evening. The meeting was scheduled over the course of three days. The sessions on the first day were directly related to my team and my expertise. The urgency to even go on this trip was now completely over as I had missed this part of the proceedings.

Admittedly, the Hertz gold star treatment was really nice. As I breezed through to my car that had been patiently waiting in the stall for me since noon, I ruefully smiled at how easy it would have been had I actually made it to the airport on time, and how my careful efforts would have actually paid off.

After checking into the hotel and getting my stuff hung up in my room, I texted one of my buddies on my team who had also flown in for the trip to see what he was doing for dinner. He was out with our IT group at a nearby restaurant and very thoughtfully invited me to join them.

I'm not sure how people jet off to places and arrive fresh-faced and rosy after hurtling through the air in everyone's stale, recycled air and slowly fizzling cologne. All I know is, after any amount of time on a plane (and I suppose in this case, additional six hours of sitting around in an airport), I feel and look like the bottom of a shoe. I changed into the casual outfit I'd brought along and went to meet my teammates at dinner.

It really was amazing to put all the faces with names. It's an odd thing to finally meet someone with whom you've spent countless hours chatting but whose hand you have never shaken; like meeting an old friend for the first time in a strange backwards reversal of time. We all had a really nice dinner.

Right before the check arrived, my buddy whipped out his iPhone to take some pics of all of us together. Having been the last one to arrive at dinner, I was seated at the end of the table closest to the camera, and it was one of those long range shots where everyone leans in to be included in the frame. The table was lit with large, overhead pendant lights in an otherwise very dim ambient glow. My hair was in its signature gone-to-the-dogs ponytail, and my makeup, so carefully applied at five AM, was now sad remnants of what could have been; smeared, smudgy artifacts of a well-intended attempt that had been long laid to waste. My stomach, having been freed of its Spanx for the first time in over fourteen hours, was having a "Just Paroled" party over the top of my pants.

I knew. I knew the picture was going to be bad.

But until I laid eyes on the permanently captured spectacle at the end of the table, all manner of pasty cellulite glaring back from under the overhead cans, hair greasy and lopsided from the wind and long day's travels, I couldn't really have realized the extent of the disaster. To say I looked like a heaping pile of lard covered dung would have been an insult to all piles of dung (heaping and otherwise) and tubs of lard respectively, across the globe. I desperately wanted to tell my friend to delete that one. However, not wanting to be *that* girl, not wanting to add "crazy" and "pathetic" to my already growing list of accolades for the day, I let it go and held my tongue.

When I got back to my hotel room, I called Russell and the kids to say goodnight. Mia answered the phone.

"Hi Mommy!" She sang into the phone.

"Hi Sweetheart! I replied. "How are you? How did school go today?"

"Fine," she said. "We had technology today. We went out to dinner tonight."

"Ooooh! You did?" I said. "Where did you go?"

"Red Lobster," she replied.

"That sounds yummy," I smiled.

"Ohhhh it was," she said. "I had mac and cheese, of course. Alex really misses you, Mom." Her tone grew softer and quieter. "And so do I."

This tugged more than a little at my heartstrings. "I know, sweetheart," I said, "I miss you guys so much. And, only two nights and I'll be home! It will go by really quickly, you'll see. I hope you have a very good night and sleep well. I love you very, very much."

"Okay Mama," she said, "Goodnight, I love you too." She handed the phone over to Alex.

"Hi my big boy!" I said brightly. "How are you?"

"Hi Mommy," came the reply. A few moments of silence.

"Did you have a good day at school today, love?" I asked him. A few more hushed moments of nothing, broken finally by the sound of sniveling.

"Where did you go, Mommy?" he sniffed. "I didn't know where you were."

"I'm in Minnesota, sweetheart," I reminded him.

"Minnesoga?" he repeated.

"Remember? I have to be here for work but only for a few days and then I'm coming right back home."

More silence.

"Will you be a brave boy and look after Mia and Daddy for me?" I asked him. I heard him sobbing on the other end of the line.

"Alex," I tried to soothe him. "Please don't cry, love. Everything's alright and I will be home very soon. I need you to help take care of Mia and Daddy, okay?"

"Okay," he finally squeaked in a very small voice and then started softly weeping again.

I just wanted to leap through the phone and hug them.

"Thank you my sweet boy," I said, as cheerfully as I could with my heart aching for my babies. "Goodnight Alex, I love you very, very much and I hope you have sweet dreams," I told him.

Russell and I spoke for a few minutes and then I let him go so he could get the kids to bed. I was completely exhausted myself. I had arranged to take my team mate to the office for the second day of sessions. The sessions were starting at eight AM, and we would meet up in the hotel lobby by seven thirty to go. I set my alarm for six AM, lay down and was out.

It was one of those sleeps where you close your eyes and seemingly seconds later, open them again and it's morning. A sleep so deep you don't recall having any dreams, and wake up in the same position as when you went to sleep, so you can't even tell if you moved at all during the night you were so tired.

The sun was streaming in through the curtains. I glanced over at the clock. Eight thirty nine. WHAT! What was that?? I bolted up and squinted at the clock, something was wrong but I was still not awake enough to really register what the problem was.

Eight thirty nine. What time zone was this again? Were we two hours ahead or behind? Then as I rapidly became more coherent I realized it didn't matter what the time zone difference was because I was here, and here it was now eight forty. And the meeting had started forty minutes ago. And I had just woken up.

My bitter cussing propelled me out of bed, almost airborne, towards the bathroom, where I stepped into a big soggy patch of carpet right next to the bathroom doorway. Ugh! What the…? I didn't have time to deal with this now, I'd obviously slopped some water onto the carpet when I'd brushed my teeth and face the night before.

While the shower was heating up I called my coworker and blurted out the situation, my alarm obviously hadn't gone off, did he get to the office? He assured me that he did and the meeting had started. I told him I'd be there as soon as I could and we hung up.

I couldn't believe it. I was positively nauseated. A missing plane part was one thing but this was totally my fault.

I flew around the room getting ready, and every time I crossed the threshold to the bathroom, I found the carpet was getting more and more soaked, the wet spot spreading outward rapidly and then noticed the large bubble under the paint over the door frame.

Well that was just absolutely perfect. On top of everything else in this ridiculous three ring circus that was pretending to be a business trip, there was now no mistaking the fact that there was a leak in the ceiling from the room above. I couldn't just ignore this.

I called the lobby and spilled the news that my room was self-installing a fountain. A member of the maintenance crew was at my door within minutes and by the time he arrived, we could literally watch the water dripping off the doorframe.

At this point, I was so late, what was another few minutes. I didn't want to risk my clothes getting drenched as well so I went down to the lobby in person to ask for a new room. The Manager was extremely responsive and immediately put me in a new room, this one was a two bedroom suite with a kitchenette and living room. It was bigger than my first apartment. She even helped me move my stuff. I thanked her profusely and set off for the meeting.

I opened the conference room door and slunk over to the closest seat, trying not to draw attention to myself but of course that was mission impossible. I crawled around on the floor plugging in my laptop, and then sank into my chair.

This part of the meeting didn't involve my team at all, so while listening in, I booted up my laptop to make sure I hadn't missed any urgent emails.

To my complete and sickening mortification, there waiting for me was an email from my friend to all of the IT team and also others in the east coast office, featuring pictures taken from the night before.

Now, not only were the people who I'd just finally met privy to the Worst Picture Ever Taken of Me, but the people who I *hadn't* met yet, who still probably had a picture of me in their minds that more closely resembled a person rather than the Swamp Thing, were made aware of this visual fiasco as well.

I went to the bathroom several hours after lunch and there in the mirror, laughing at me while I washed my hands, was a large piece of spinach stuck in my teeth. Of course. I wasn't even fazed at this point. The only thing left would be to walk out with toilet paper stuck to my shoe or fart accidentally in the next session or something.

That night I set my alarm, placed a wakeup call and set the room clock alarm. I stopped myself from deciding to sleep with the window open and asking the fire department to please hose down my bedroom window at six AM the next morning just in case the other three methods failed to retrieve me again from the Land of Nod.

The third day actually went well and due to an ad-hoc added session, I got to provide some relevant input for a few hours.

But the damage was done. I was beaten. This trip had cut me down to size and I was feeling very small indeed. It was a dejected and weary Romi who arrived back at the airport to wait for the return flight home.

However. The funny thing about life is that sometimes, in the midst of a major karmic smack down, you will get an incredible break. It just so happens that of all the trips and all the airports, of all the gates and all the timing, another one of my best friends and her daughter happened to be connecting through Minnesota on their way to Boston.

This friend lives in Vegas, so we don't get to see each other that often, and between our recent work schedules and various other factors, hadn't seen each other in nearly a year. Through a series of texts we arranged to meet up outside the G gates.

We literally had five stolen minutes before they had to go so they wouldn't miss their connecting flight. It was such an amazing bonus to see them at all, and made all the preceding days' events well worth the agony.

When I dragged my depleted self through the front door close to midnight, the security system chime woke up Alex. He ran out of the bedroom to the top of the stairs and was so half asleep and overcome to see me that he just burst out crying and crumpled into a heap at the landing. I scooped him up into my arms and rubbed his back. His cries woke up Mia, who came bounding out of her bedroom and promptly began bawling as well.

"It's okay," I whispered, hugging them both to me, feeling their tears running down my neck into my shirt, "Mommy's home."

ME TOO

Me too. The song of the subsequent born.

The five year gap between my two children means that sometimes finding the balance between such different ages and stages is a chasm that is not always bridgeable.

Alex just wants to be like his big sister and join in the fun. Now that he's three and finally big enough to keep up with her a little more, there are times when this is absolutely doable, like when we cook up homemade pancakes on the weekend. Mia has been my kitchen helper for years, and suddenly now there are four extra hands mixing, cracking eggs and spilling drops of milk from the measuring cup on its wobbly way to the bowl.

I watch the siblings next to each other, Alex standing on one of the kitchen chairs, his little toes gripping the leather of the seat cushion for extra stability, and Mia right next to him, trying to help him stir while he tries to do it all himself. Their shoulders touch while they work; two bookends operating in unison, their little scapulae moving gracefully in their small backs. Sometimes they look at each other and laugh, sometimes they bicker over who gets to do what. These moments make me completely happy, they are so sweet and priceless.

When packages arrive, my kids love to make little houses or forts out of the boxes. Mia is usually the first to grab the biggest box.

"I'm going to make a cat bed!" she'll exclaim and take her prize off to the living room to get started.

"Me too!" yells Alex, following her.

"I have one for you," Mia will assure her brother, and disappears off to the recycling pile in the garage to find a suitable match. They push them next to each other, and, having stuffed them full of blankets and pillows, curl up next to each other, meowing and purring. This usually lasts for a few minutes before Alex can't contain himself anymore and leaps out of the box, suddenly metamorphosed into a dinosaur, or Mia starts fussing with him too much and he screeches and runs away.

But sometimes, the prospect at hand is not a team sport.

When Mia began to have play dates and sleepovers, suddenly Alex's playmate was off limits from time to time. I have very mixed feelings about this; I think Mia should learn to include her little brother even though it means that he won't be able to play all the games and she and her friends need to be considerate and mindful of what he is capable of doing. However at the same time, Mia also needs to be able to play with friends of her own vintage, and play all the games that are age appropriate for them.

Mia's friend came over last weekend for a play

date. Her mom and I chatted for a bit while all three kids ran around the living room laughing and chasing each other.

After the other mom left, Mia and friend started heading upstairs to her room.

"Me too!" Alex yelled, his face consumed with panic as the two girls cleared the landing, running behind them in hot pursuit.

"Come here, Alex," I tried to coax him, "I have a new game for us to play!" He continued charging up the stairs, totally ignoring me. I ran upstairs after him, wanting desperately to shield my boy from this disappointment and simultaneously wanting to give Mia her time with her friend to do their thing.

"No, Alex!" Mia bellowed, trying to close the door as Alex wrestled her on the other side of it, "This is just for big girls!!"

"ME TOO!" Alex shrieked, pushing back so that she couldn't close it.

"Love, come downstairs with me, let's let the girls play," I tried again. "We'll play our own game."

"No! I want to play with the gewls!" He protested angrily, frantically banging on the door as it was shut in his face, "Let me in, Miaaaaaa!"

He slumped to the floor outside her closed bedroom door and his bereft face, distorted in a frozen, defeated grimace, was agony for me to witness. There was no sound; just huge tears spilling out of his pained eyes. These were not the tears of a childish tantrum; they were big, hurt tears of rejection and there was really nothing I could do to ease them.

As the second born, this is his bitter lesson to learn. Sometimes his big sister needs her space and her time to herself, and he can't always join in too.

I picked him up and the fight was gone, he put his head on my shoulder and sobbed, his little arms clasped tightly around my neck. I hugged him tightly in return and rubbed his back as I carefully carried him back downstairs. I tried to distract him with puzzles, Lego and cars but every so often when I let down my guard he ran back upstairs to try his luck, only to get the proverbial kick in the teeth again.

Alex and I have very little one on one time. Due to the way the day times out, he often has to share my attention with Mia. So now that he was older, when Mia was invited over to friends' houses for playdates, I thought we would finally have some time to spend together, just the two of us.

This time, while he wasn't directly the brunt of a door in his face, Alex would get so upset to drop his sister off and drive away without her that he would cry himself to sleep and spend the whole afternoon passed out, napping.

The first time this happened, I was very disappointed as well. I had placed so much importance on the afternoon and was so looking forward to having that bonding time with my boy. Alex is so sleep deprived most of the time though and badly needed the slumber, so I just let those rare afternoons slip by, grateful that at least he was having a really good nap.

But recently, Mia was invited to a party that would span most of the afternoon. It was a girls-only bash, and I got the message: Alex wasn't invited. This time, Alex fell asleep in the car on the way to drop her off. I drove around for a while, letting him snooze. Alex is terrified of the car wash and I really, really had to get it done. He didn't even stir as we were shuffled along, the water pelting on the roof and roar of the scrubbers were no match for his exhaustion.

After about an hour, he bolted up in his car seat and blinked furiously. "Where's Mia?" he asked, looking at her empty booster.

"She's at a party, love," I answered, looking at him in the rear view mirror, "But you and I are going to have a special Alex-Mommy play date today. Just you and I."

He broke into a smile, eyes wide in surprise. "A play date?"

"Yes," I smiled back. "You and I can go wherever you like today. What do you want to do?"

He thought about it for a second. "Cow train!" was the response.

The cow train is Alex's favorite ride at the pumpkin patch, and we recently discovered another version of it at the Wooden Shoe Tulip Festival in Woodburn. It's a train made of sideways hollowed out industrial steel storage drums on wheels, complete with faces and handles for ears, and each drum is painted to look like a slightly different Holstein. The whole thing is whipped along by a tractor going as fast as possible around a dirt track. At Wooden Shoe it actually takes you right through the tulip beds as well.

Alex still likes me to go on the ride with him, so I get down into Bessie's muddy belly and he clamors onto my lap. I hold onto Alex while he holds onto the handles, and away we go, bumping and jolting through the fields. Doing donuts in the dust and bouncing along in a frenzy of muck flinging figure eights is not my typical pastime but the continuous stream of hysterical giggling from my boy makes it my favorite ride at the pumpkin patch too.

"The cow train isn't running today," I told my boy. "It's only May and we won't be able to go on it for a while. What else should we do?"

"The park!" he countered.

"The park it is!" I agreed, watching his smile broaden in the mirror. It was an absolutely beautiful day, not even a wisp of cloud breaking the azure sky, and the sun felt like heaven on our northwestern arms and legs. Alex ran, jumped and climbed, totally in his element.

"Let's go on the swings, Mommy!" he said, dashing for the swing set. I had to help him get onto this one as it was just a little too high for him to climb on by himself.

"Are you ready?" I prompted, pulling the swing backwards.

"YES!" he shouted.

"Hold on with both hands," I reminded him, "And if you want to stop, tell me, don't just jump off, okay?"

"Okay!" he confirmed gleefully.

I let the swing go and he went flying, his little brown Merrells sailing into the sky. I pushed him higher and higher until he called out, "That's enough, Mommy." I watched his small body moving to and fro, his head back, huge grin on his face. Being three is so sublime; feeling the air rushing past your face, without a care in the world. It made me smile at the joy of being a parent and getting to experience it all over again with my son.

When he was done swinging, Alex wanted to leave the park. "Let's go see some fishies, Mommy!" He announced.

"Sure," I obliged. I took him to a local pet shop to look at the fish, and there happened to be a pet rescue taking place outside. We stayed outside for a while, looking at the forlorn little puppies. I was surprised that Alex didn't ask to take one home; if Russell had been with us we probably would have come home with twelve new furry family members. Inside the store, Alex got to see the fish, birds and hamsters and even touch a lizard. His eyes were sparkling as we left the store.

"Where should we go now?" I asked. This was Alex's day. I left it entirely up to him.

"Mmmmm," he pondered, "How 'bout frozen

yogurt?"

"That sounds wonderful, love!" I agreed. "Let's go!"

When we got to the frozen yogurt store, Alex took a cup for himself and handed me one as well. I was touched by this chivalrous little gesture. He turned his attention to the flavors on the machines.

For Alex, frozen yogurt is a misnomer. Frozen toppings would sum it up more accurately. True to form, he wildly dispensed a blob of watermelon sorbet into his cup and then darted over to the topping bar.

"Oooooh, I want pinkles, Mom!" He squealed.

"You can have sprinkles, love," I said, scooping a small spoonful of them onto his yogurt.

"And cocolit cips!"

I obliged with the chocolate chips.

"And gummy worms!"

I had to put the kibosh on the gummy worms so that my cupped palm wouldn't end up having to be the receptacle for them, half chewed and drooly, in about five minutes. "These are really sour, Alex, you don't like these."

"And pink!" He layered a generous spoonful of salmon colored boba balls over the chocolate chips.

"Alright," I said, ushering us along before my child ended up with a sixteen ounce cup of candy to wolf down, "That looks really yummy, sweetheart! Let's go pay and have our froyo."

"Deal!" he exclaimed, giving me the thumbs up

and winking at me.

We sat outside and ate our desserts in hushed happiness. Alex slid down off his chair and climbed up onto my lap.

"I love you, Mommy," he said, giving me a sticky bear hug.

"I love you so much too, Alex!" I told him, hugging him in return and kissing him on his head.

He pulled back a little so that he could see my face. "Are you still my best friend?" he asked.

I looked into his sepia brown eyes. "I will *always* be your best friend, my sweet boy, no matter what."

He gave me a dazzling grin, his crimson sprinkled yogostache framing his beautiful, straight teeth.

We hit Build a Bear and Stride Rite as well before calling it quits to go and pick up Mia. All in all, we'd had a pretty full afternoon. To be honest, none of the things we'd done were earth-shatteringly new or bucket list type of items. In that day I hadn't taught my son to read; we hadn't solved world peace or gone hang-gliding or hot air ballooning. But this unhurried time with Alex was the real magic in itself; the point wasn't *where* we were spending this time together but rather *that* we were spending it together. Instead of trying to create the Instagram-worthy perfect day for my boy I had just let go of the reins, and he had showed me the best time of all.

I studied Alex in the rear view mirror again as we pulled up in front of the birthday girl's driveway.

"Thank you for a really wonderful play date, Alex," I told him, "I had so much fun with you today."

He caught my eye in the mirror and beamed back at me. "Me too," he concurred.

DEAR MIA AND ALEX

My Dearest Children,

Right now you are nine and three. One teetering on the cusp of tweenhood and the other ready to close the door on his toddlerhood.

Already it is going so fast; as cliché as it sounds, it really does seem that just yesterday your Dad and I were bringing you home from the hospital, all tiny and fresh.

Then it seemed that you would be babies forever, that I would always feel your formula-scented breath against my neck as you slept, curled into a soft, warm ball on my chest, your teeny eyelids fluttering as you dreamed your sweet infant dreams full of nothing but promises of the world that awaited you. It felt like I would always be able to drink in your huge, toothless smiles and delicious baby chortles; that our eyes would always lock in a gaze so intense and filled with love that it would make me catch my breath.

I remember packing away the size 2T clothes that I got for the baby showers and thinking it would be such a long time before you got big enough to wear them. Yet wasn't it the next week when I was packing them away again, this time to donate as you'd already outgrown them.

The milestones are sometimes big and glaring, like turning one, that first word, first step, first tooth, first lost tooth. But sometimes they are quieter: when you learned to fasten a button or lather a soap or sing or pop a puzzle piece in the right way.

As you mature you will find that you continue to reach milestones in yet other unexpected ways; when you learn how to truly forgive and how to give to others without any expectation of anything in return, when you learn to truly enjoy your own company.

When I was younger I used to fret about how I would leave my mark on this world, how I would leave something of myself behind so that once I am gone, there will still be proof that I was here and that I gave something meaningful to this world. I no longer worry about this, as my legacy is you.

As you grow, my babies, there will be blissful days where all is right with the world and you are happy and useful and in your element. These will be days where you can do no wrong, and they will make you feel wonderful and glad that you are alive. On these days you will be the hero, you may even win trophies or awards, people will give you compliments and want to be around you. You will shine.

As much as it pains me to even write this, you

will have bad days too. There will be people who won't understand you, who will try to break you or dim your light for no other reason than they can't see their own, who will make fun of you and call you names, or laugh at what you're wearing or belittle you because of something you said, or even how you said it. There will be people who won't like you for no apparent reason at all.

And as sad as this will make you feel, you will have no idea that my heart will be breaking tenfold for you, because I see all the amazing potential within you and because I see you through eyes of a love so deep and so unconditional that I can't fathom how someone else could look at you any other way.

While I want so desperately to shield you from all the painful days that will inevitably come your way, I know these lessons are yours to learn and they must come in order to shape you. They will make you the person you are to become.

Remember that on the days when you feel blue and despondent and that you can't like yourself even a little bit, I will like you enough for both of us.

Remember that you can't win them all, and sometimes the struggle wasn't yours to fight in the first place.

Remember that your moment of victory is someone else's moment to lose. Be a humble and gracious winner.

Remember your good manners and your common sense, even when it's not "cool" to do so, or even if your friends have forgotten theirs.

Remember that everyone is somebody's baby. Please be kind to them. And I pray with all my soul that they will be kind to you.

One day, you will learn that even on the bad days there is so much good, and you are still glad to be alive and that you are still strong and unique and amazing.

And most importantly, remember that through it all, I will be there for you any time you should ever need me. I will always root for you, no matter what.

You are beautiful, my babies, and you are so, so loved.

Mom

ACKNOWLEDGEMENTS

A gigantic thank you to Amy Hansen for her continued editing and guidance to get this book into its final polished form. A huge thank you to the talented Deborah Bradseth of Tugboat Design for the cover design.

Thank you so much Katie Schneider for your invaluable help with formatting.

Thank you to every boss I've ever had for not firing me over the ridiculous things I have managed to do while under their employ.

Thank you to every reader who has picked up this book and taken a gamble to share in these experiences with me.

Mom and Dad, now I get it. Thank you for not just dropping me off somewhere and not coming back for me when I was driving you nuts.

Thank you to my husband and my children, for the continued support and endless inspiration. I love you more than you will ever know.

Check out my other book:
Please Tell Me I'm On Mute

For more information, find me at:

Twitter: @RomiBrennerBook
Facebook: Romi Brenner

www.ingramcontent.com/pod-product-compliance
Lightning Source LLC
Chambersburg PA
CBHW061820040426
42447CB00012B/2738